P9-DGZ-018

YOUR COMPETITIVE EDGE

YOUR COMPETITIVE EDGE

How to Attract, Optimize, and Hold Your Best Employees

Roger E. Herman, CSP, CMC
Joyce L. Gioia, CMC

And the Fellows of The
Workforce Stability Institute

Published under the sponsorship of
The Workforce Stability Institute by

OAKHILL PRESS
Winchester, Virginia

10   9   8   7   6   5   4   3   2   1

Library of Congress Cataloging-in-Publication Data

Herman, Roger E., 1943–
    Workforce Stability: your competitive edge: how to attract, optimize, and hold your best employees / Roger E. Herman, Joyce L. Gioia
       p. cm.
    Includes bibliographical references and index.
    ISBN 1-886939-36-5
    1. Incentives in industry—United States   2. Career development—United States.   3. Compensation management—United States.   I. Gioia, Joyce L. (Joyce Leah), 1947–   II. Title.
HF5549.5.I5 H4674 2000
658.3—dc21   00-21843
                               CIP

Oakhill Press
461 Layside Drive
Winchester, VA 22602
800-32-Books
Printed in the United States of America

Dedication

We are pleased and honored to dedicate this book to the legions of hard-working human resource professionals who toil daily in a valiant effort to build stability, harmony, and productivity in workplaces throughout the world.

The field of human resources is changing, continuing the transformation from "personnel" administration to a highly sophisticated strategic role in the corporate arena. The profession is becoming more exciting, challenging, and influential.

In this fast-changing environment, professionals need resources, guidance, and coordination. We salute The Society for Human Resource Management, the leading organization in the field, for the great work being done to support the people who make things work for their employers.

The years ahead will be filled with challenges as the competition for good workers intensifies. We acknowledge the work that will be done by human resource professionals to enable their employers to become more stable, productive, and meaningful.

6-8-00

Contents

Acknowledgments

The creation of *Workforce Stability* has been a collaborative effort. We thank each of the Fellows of the Workforce Stability Institute for their professional contributions. Each of these people has valuable expertise in their areas of specialty. We appreciate them sharing their knowledge and perspectives. Contributors are recognized as their chapters are introduced and you can learn more about them from the biographical profiles at the end of this book.

The staffs of the Workforce Stability Institute and The Herman Group are due a great vote of appreciation for their support as this book came together. Thanks especially to Carol McKinney, Kim Bauer, Mark Funkhouser, and Cindy Boren.

A special salute goes to Drew Perry, a fine editor working with the Workforce Stability Institute. His efforts in bringing things together were instrumental in our achieving our goals for this educational project.

The professionals at Oakhill Press deserve accolades as well. Thanks to Ed Helvey, Paula Gould, and BJ Gardner. We again acknowledge the fine work of Craig Hines of Bellerophon Productions, one of the finest typesetters and book designers around.

Finally, thanks to all the clients of the Institute and its Fellows who have provided valuable feedback, critique, and practical application regarding the workforce stability model. Everyone working together can indeed make a positive difference.

Introduction

In these turbulent times, unstable conditions make it more difficult to achieve corporate goals and earn a profit or serve constituents. Whatever can be done to build stability is a positive move.

The greatest investment—or operating expense—in most organizations is the cost of attracting, optimizing, and holding competent employees. Successful employers maximize the return on their investments in human resources. A well-trained, dedicated, long-tenured workforce facilitates the continuity that enables an organization to realize its full potential.

The stability of the workforce, then, is clearly a competitive advantage in today's world.

Workforce stability doesn't just happen. Since there are so many other employers competing for the same people you want to employ, it's not a natural phenomenon. Deliberate strategic steps must be taken to achieve stability. Simply hiring more people through the revolving door of the employment department is not the answer. Throwing more money at people won't keep them around, either. A comprehensive approach is needed.

To build the stability of your workforce, there are a number of improvements to make in the way you are recruiting, selecting, hiring, orienting, training, utilizing, and retaining people. Each of the areas of concern is a component of a model developed by the Workforce Stability Institute to assure that all aspects of workforce stability are addressed.

The chapters that follow in this book will each explore one of the components of the model, explaining its importance, essentials of its composition, and some ideas on practical things employers can and—in our opinion—should do. The book is not meant to provide all the answers and all the how-to's about workforce stability. To meet that objective would require a much larger volume than *Workforce Stability*.

Our purpose in this book is to introduce the model, to stimulate your thinking, and to give you greater insight into what should be done to build your workforce stability. Our Fellows stand ready to assist you in going deeper into the various aspects of building stability in your organization. Contact us at 336-282-1480 or info@employee.org.

1

Today's Predicament

Roger Herman, CSP, CMC

We live in interesting times. The ancient curse has become a reality. The workforce conditions of today—and tomorrow—are unprecedented.

Everyone involved in running a business, government organization, or nonprofit agency faces challenges for which no one is prepared. It's a whole new ball game—with new rules, new players, and a much different playing field. The traditional methods that have worked in the past don't seem to work as well today.

Human resource professionals, company owners, senior executives, department heads—managers and leaders at all levels and at all types of employers find it substantially more difficult to recruit, optimize, and retain qualified workers.

What's Causing This Predicament?

The severe labor shortage we are now experiencing has been building for quite a while. It's not new. We knew this was coming. Back in 1990 we forecasted an unprecedented churning in the labor market, warning that it would begin mid-decade. The churning continues, and will continue for at least the first decade of the 21st century.

There are a number of underlying causes for this turbulence. Let's explore a few, so we can better understand what's happening around us. First, we are in the midst of an extraordinary economic expansion. The economists we counsel with, in corporate and independent positions, forecast that the current boom conditions will continue until 2010–2012. This ongoing economic strength means that more jobs will be created, even beyond our present high levels.

Second, technology is developing rapidly, forever changing the way many jobs are performed. While this application of technology is important from a productivity perspective, it's almost overwhelming from a labor perspective. Now, employers must hire workers with higher levels of technological competency, raising the caliber of people who must be recruited, trained, and put to work.

Third, a 15 percent drop in the birth rate from a generation ago means we have fewer new entrants to the labor force than we've had in the past. Moving from the Baby Boomers, at 76.4 million people, to Generation X, at 68.5 million, creates a large reduction in the flow of recent high school and college graduates into the workforce. Since we can't manufacture more people, we have a clear supply and demand problem. Future birth rate numbers don't offer a lot of promise for significant alleviation of this shortage.

To counteract this shortage of traditional flows into the workforce, employers have tapped more and more into nontraditional workers: retirees, former military personnel, chronically unemployed persons, the physically and mentally challenged, displaced homemakers, and even the folks that some euphemistically refer to as "the homeless and the unwashed." In a full employment economy, even those who would not normally work have wonderful opportunities.

Heightened Competition for Desired Employees

Without sufficient people to fill the jobs, the labor shortage will persist and probably intensify. The competition for qualified employees will be the paramount issue facing every employer for at least a decade. This problem won't go away, so we need to confront it head-on with new approaches and new strategies. Our response must be comprehensive, not piecemeal. It must be decisive and long-term, not wishy-washy and temporary. A quick fix will not work. Inconsistency across internal organizational lines will not work.

To compete today, for the long term, employers must engage this challenge, this opportunity, from the top of the organization. The top executives must be involved—not just committed, but involved as role models, as cheerleaders, and as active supporters of all the initiatives that will be undertaken by their people. Workforce stability will be the competitive advantage for employers, so this work is clearly strategic in nature.

Workforce Stability

Workforce stability. It means exactly what it sounds like. Not continual recruitment. Not hiring one "warm body" after another. Not a revolving door employment office. Stability. Continuity. A solid workforce of people who know what they're doing, are dedicated to serving customers and who are with their employer for the long haul. Deliberately. Intentionally.

Building a stable, productive workforce in a societal environment that condones and even encourages frequent movement between jobs won't be easy. Many forces will work against success of even the most valiant efforts. But, it can be done. Stability can be achieved.

Let's accept that there are degrees of stability. A 100 percent stable workforce may not be a desired goal. Most leaders agree that a regular infusion of "new blood" is energizing for any organization. How close to 100 percent should you come? That's a strategic decision for each employer to make. Many will suggest that the goal should be 100 percent, with new people coming through growth instead of as replacements for those who depart.

Whatever goal you set, achieving it will place your organization in a considerably stronger position than you are in today. You will enjoy a competitive advantage that will drive more dollars to your bottom line because you won't be squandering money on continual recruiting, hiring, training, team-building, and reinforcing positive behaviors. You'll invest in long-term employees, building their capacity, performance, and satisfaction. Your investment will return gratifying dividends and you'll sleep well at night. And so will your employees.

Building Workforce Stability

Leaders seeking to build stability cannot operate in an intellectual vacuum. You must be keenly aware of the world around you. Specifically, we believe it is essential that you are familiar with workforce and workplace trends. Our workforce is changing. It is different today than yesterday, and will be even more different tomorrow. To adequately prepare for tomorrow, you should know what tomorrow will look like . . . and what tomorrow's workforce will look like. New workers will think differently, have different expectations—and those attitudes will, to a certain extent, be adopted by those currently in the workforce.

Under changing conditions, the staffing process itself is prone to significant change. Your approaches will become more strategic, less reactionary. You will certainly be less responsive to applicants who simply show up at the door looking for a job. Everyone will be involved in the effort to find the right people and bring them into the organization, and every new employee will be treated specially because of who he or she is. The entire process will be focused on bringing people on for an extended period of employment, rather than expecting people to leave.

Selection Processes and Tools

For each hire, you will know exactly what you are looking for, from a long-term as well as a short-term perspective. Your objective will be to build and enhance your organization's capacity for the work to be done—today and tomorrow. People will be invited to join you because of their present attitudes and skills, as well as their interest and aptitude in growth of their careers and your plans as well. Again, this design will be strategic, based in part on where your company intends to go in the years ahead.

Your selection process will become much more sophisticated. It will begin with a much clearer recognition of what you're looking for, the establishment of more exacting criteria, and a commitment to hire only those people who fit with the culture and mesh with their prospective co-workers. Line managers, not just human resource professionals, will support this orientation toward hiring people who are congruent with the company's values and mission. Attitudes about the people standards will be ubiquitous.

Human resource professionals will be highly conversant with selection tools and their applications—for hiring as well as for assigning and promoting people within the organization. You will be keenly aware of selection technologies and will pick those that will be best for your organization. Even with all the activity and clamor about selection, you will be highly focused on what's best for you. Of course, your research will continue, and you'll stay alert for developments in the field that may enhance your capability.

Recognizing that the people you want may not be easy to find, you'll mount a deliberate campaign to attract the applicants you desire. Recruiting will be highly targeted, concentrating on identifying and inviting specific people to join your organization. Your employment marketing effort will resemble an institutional marketing campaign, a branding effort for your company and the opportunities you offer. Technology will come into play, using Internet and telephonic screening to narrow the field. Marketing professionals will work hand-in-hand with human resource professionals to send clear and consistent messages through a variety of media.

Humanizing the Selection Process

The hiring process is a human experience: people hiring people. Your human resource professionals and all your managers involved in hiring will be well-trained and equipped to engage in highly productive two-way interviewing. They will gain a considerable amount of information from the applicant, while answering every question posed by the applicant. Their communication with the applicant will include what they learn from professional sales training—meeting objectives and closing the sale. Relationship building will begin during this process, focusing on prospective employees joining the employer for a long time.

In order to enhance and support the human-to-human aspects of hiring, computer-based technologies will be utilized. To strengthen the effectiveness of the hiring process, computers will guide the interchange of information and build consistency into the experience. Technology will be used in the initial screening process to support first-level evaluation of applicants. Those who pass through to the next level may well be interviewed using the aid of a computer that can suggest specific questions to ask based on the applicant's background and data furnished during the interview. These technologies will take the screening and hiring process to a new level, differentiating sophisticated employers from those who will hire "from the gut."

Retaining Employees After They Come Aboard

Once the applicant is hired, the relationship building will begin in earnest. During the orientation and bonding period, the new employee will learn about the industry, the company, and the people. Over a period of several weeks, the new member of the family will learn about the employer's history, mission, leaders, and facilities. They'll meet people, tour facilities, and become wholly immersed in the organization and its culture. Emotional bonds will begin to build, similar to those engendered in a courtship. Orientation will be much more than just filling out some forms and watching an old video.

Very early in the new employee's tenure, he or she will sit down with the supervisor and someone from the human resource or training department. An individualized career development plan will be constructed, with specific learning experiences scheduled for the first 6 or twelve months. The supervisor will commit to supporting the new employee in this growth process, which will be good for the employer as well as the worker. The message will be very clear: we expect you to be here for quite a while, so we're going to make an investment in you.

Training for retention will be a strong strategy. Employers will offer training and education programs in-house, will bring in outside professional trainers under contract, will send employees to courses and seminars at community colleges and universities, and will send people to educational sessions sponsored by trade associations. You'll offer tuition reimbursement, cross-training, and special assignments. Mentoring and coaching programs will provide personal growth, enabling each employee to develop on his or her own schedule . . . supported by the employer.

Providing Support

Recognizing that not all employees are natural high achievers, employers will provide special assistance for those who need a little extra help. Through this investment, under-achievers will have opportunities to reach more of their potential, then raise their own levels of growth and performance. These workers—at all levels in the organization—will sincerely appreciate the efforts of their employer to help them, and they'll tend to stay longer and perform with a greater sense of purpose.

Front-line workers are the heartbeat of any organization. To build workforce stability, you'll work extra diligently with these valuable people to make them feel a part of what's happening with the company. They'll gain a deeper understanding of their role, of the company's operations, and of how they can help the company—and themselves—succeed. This energizing of the front-line personnel will have many positive effects on the organization as a whole.

Communication

Keeping people informed and involved will be accomplished through a process best described as Internal Marketing. You'll apply the proven principles of marketing for customers to win the interest, engagement, and loyalty of your internal customers—your employees. A wide range of communications media will be used to reach your workers and their families, strengthening the bonds that hold people to their employer.

Recognition for performance and retention will play a major role in building stability. You'll recognize and award individual performers, teams, departments, and entire companies. Special occasions, worthy performance, and special talents and contributions will all be saluted, adding to the joy and value of working for you. The recognition process and culture will bring a special excitement to the workplace that will energize people and the environment in which they work.

Employee retention efforts will be far-reaching, with all managers dedicated to practicing the principles of leadership that inspire people to stay with an employer. With acknowl-

edgment that the worker's relationship with his or her immediate supervisor is paramount, retention efforts will focus on
creating and maintaining the optimal organizational culture,
valuing each person, providing support, enabling growth and
development, and compensating fairly. Managers will be
trained and supported to take appropriate steps to retain people by giving them what they need to be successful on and
off the job.

Leadership Responsibilities

Leadership makes a difference in building workforce stability as well. The traditional styles of management, taught and
reinforced for years, will not be sufficient or appropriate in
the stable environment. Rather than managing or leading
groups or teams, leaders will practice "facilitative leadership"—facilitating the high performance of each individual.

New principles of leadership will come into play, giving
workers more freedom and flexibility to get the job done.
Greater autonomy, power, and accountability will characterize the new design.

Workforce stability will indeed be your competitive edge.
As you move forward, building greater degrees of stability,
your performance will reflect your success. Before your
competitors know what has happened, you'll be in an envi-
able position of having the people who can get the job done
. . . and get it done well and on time. As other employers
struggle to get enough people to even fill the positions, you'll
be solid, productive, and profitable.

In order to begin to understand how to gain the competitive edge
that workforce stability will provide, you must first understand
certain basic characteristics about the workforce itself. Carol
D'Amico, an expert on workforce trends and development, tackles

the issues inherent in America's changing workforce and offers forecasts and predictions for the 21st century. D'Amico is a nationally known lecturer, advisor, and consultant and regularly speaks and publishes on subjects such as leadership, economic and educational policy, and program development. Her chapter will outline some of the trends we see in today's employee market and will address ways employers can combat a declining availability of qualified employees.

2

Our Changing Workforce

Carol D'Amico, Ph.D.

Factors Affecting American Corporations

In order to understand the concept of workforce stability, you must first understand the makeup of the workforce you are seeking to stabilize. The face of the American workforce today is different than it has been at any time in our history, and it is changing almost daily as factors such as technology and globalization come more and more to the fore. Employers seeking to add new hires and expand their business are discovering that the market for new employees is tighter than they had expected. And if the market is tight today, just wait: as Baby Boomers exit the workforce and the growth rate of the incoming labor force slows, the market will get even tighter. The big news, in fact, for American employers over the next 10–20 years is not necessarily the changing demographics of race and gender, but of age. The four key factors affecting employers today are

- the changing demographic composition of the workers
- the need for increasingly skilled workers
- the alarming increase of ill-equipped employees
- the changing workplace, which will require missing skills

Demographics

The ethnic makeup of the labor force is not really changing as much as you might think. The U.S. Bureau of Statistics does indeed forecast a nearly 10 percent increase in the number of minority workers in the workforce over the next 20 years, but these increases are spread among various ethnic groups so evenly as to make for a very slight change in the overall picture. The workforce over the next 20 or so years will continue to be approximately 70 percent white, with the remaining workers being about 15 percent Hispanic, 10 percent black, and 5 percent Asian and others. These percentages do not mean that the special needs of these workers should not be addressed, but for those looking to grasp the larger picture of the evolving workforce, these numbers do not really represent a significant change.

As well, while in 1995 the workforce was split 45 percent female to 55 percent male, in 2020 the Bureau predicts that the market will be split 50–50 between men and women. Again, this change is not insignificant, but these numbers do not reflect a drastic change in workforce makeup.

The age makeup of the workforce, however, will be of increasing importance as Baby Boomers retire and so-called Gen-Xers move increasingly slowly to take their places. Whereas in 1995 only 9 percent of the workforce was 55–64 years of age, in 2020 that number is predicted to be 20 percent or higher. As well, the number of younger workers is showing a higher and higher level of decrease. The Bureau predicts only an 11 percent increase in the labor force from 1996 to 2006. That rate is only half of what it was from 1976 to 1986. This rate of growth will be the lowest since the 1960's and 1970's.

New Skills Needed in the Modern Workplace

Three-quarters of all new jobs are in the professional, managerial, and technical fields. The skills required for these jobs are obviously quite high-level. As production and agricultural jobs are on the decline, high-tech jobs are naturally on the rise. Today's hyper-paced information age requires that workers be proficient in a variety of skills, from communication to technology to marketing and managing. The fragmenting marketplace requires more and more individual ability. The old paradigm of spending 50 years doing essentially the same thing is obsolete.

The computer and data processing sectors alone are forecast to increase by 108 percent over the next 20 years, adding 1.3 million jobs. One needs only to read the front page of any business paper or magazine to get a sense of the scope of today's technology-based market; almost every day another "dot com" business launches, and a slew of support businesses are born weekly to assist all the "dot coms." A new understanding of the intricacies of technology, of business, and of people will be required of both management and new hires.

Employees Entering the Workforce
Lack Vital Knowledge

In 1996, the U.S. Department of Education reported that almost 40 percent of the adult population in America was fundamentally illiterate in math skills, reading, and document analysis. Employers everywhere are reporting anecdotal evidence of a consistent decline in the quality of their new workers. Combine the forecast shortage in quantity of workers with the existing and worsening shortage of quality workers, and you can see that trouble not only looms on the horizon, but is already upon us. What will employers do when they either can't find anyone to hire or discover that those people they do hire are nearly incompetent?

There is a marked shortage of the people we need in America. While the numbers of employees with four-year degrees are holding almost steady, the numbers of people with semi-skilled degrees are declining drastically. As the need for skilled workers increases almost exponentially with the rise in technology-based business, a workforce crunch the likes of which we have never seen is building. In short, the education levels and job requirements of new positions are rising, and the quality of workers available to fill those positions is falling.

Six out of ten companies report serious deficiencies in basic job attitudes and abilities among their workers. Half of today's companies say their employees lack the ability to read and translate drawings, diagrams, and flow charts. And don't be fooled: The Department of Education suggests that even those people holding four-year degrees may be slipping through the cracks—14 percent to 16 percent of college graduates have been found to be functionally illiterate.

What's more, in today's globalized economy, America's young people—the workforce of tomorrow—simply aren't measuring up to their peers in other countries. The U.S. graduation rate of 72 percent is second to last—outranking only Mexico—among industrial nations. As the economy goes more and more global, if the educational levels of tomorrow's labor pool are not up to the standard of workers available outside the United States, it will become difficult—if not impossible—to keep jobs in the country. There is simply an extraordinary shortage of both existing and entering qualified employees in today's market.

Adding It All Up

So what does it all mean? How will you survive, given the bleak prospects outlined above? You must find ways to train employees already in your employ as well as those who will be joining your firm in the coming years. More importantly, you *must* retain those employees who can function and allow you to compete in the marketplace.

Employers need to recognize their needs early on and design training and retention programs based upon those needs. Employers need to:

- Identify skill levels needed for any given job, and recruit accordingly
- Offer training opportunities so that employees may learn and acquire those skills in a user-friendly and effective environment
- Understand those skills and skill levels, and understand how and when to combat perceived deficiencies
- Examine demographic profiles in order to gain knowledge about where and how to recruit the most valuable, best-equipped workers
- Adopt systemic processes to retain those workers of high skill and quality
- Design a work environment which sustains and encourages the use of existing and developing technologies for jobs
- Adopt retention plans specific to different types of workers
- Adopt benefits packages specific to different types of workers

Acting Now

You must act upon these trends now, not react to them years from now. If you wait to change the way your company pursues and retains employees until you find that you must do so in order to keep up with the competition, it will be too late. As the growth of the workforce slows and the quality of the workforce declines, employers will be in increasingly tight competition for the best employees. Tactics such as marketing the company to potential employees, new hiring systems, career development and education, training, and innovations in recognition and reward will have to be implemented in order to survive.

The "how-tos" of survival in the 21st-century workforce are explored in detail in coming chapters. You must design proactive retention and hiring systems in order to survive. Look around you, at your old employees and at your new hires. Consider the costs of losing your qualified people. Consider the costs of being unable to replace them. Act now to ensure you don't have to consider these things in a far more concrete way.

Obviously, a key factor—perhaps the key factor—in finding the right employee is figuring out how to hire the people you need. In the coming chapter, Wayne Outlaw, a nationally acclaimed business writer and theorist, explores ways to plan and build your staffing process in a holistic manner. He looks at ways to establish the most successful, effective, and efficient means of selection available within the staffing process. The purpose of this analysis is to transfer the benefits gained in finding the right employee to the bottom line. Outlaw suggests that innovative and successful staffing will increase the success and health of any company.

3

The Strategic Staffing Process

Wayne Outlaw, CSP, CMC

A Holistic Approach for Better Organizational Results

In years past, many organizations felt that there was an ample labor pool to provide an unending supply of employees for their human capital needs. They believed that even if employees left, personnel simply placed an ad in the paper and easily filled the position. This situation does not exist today, nor will it exist in the foreseeable future. Between now and the year 2005, the reduction of workers entering the workforce will increase the number of unfilled jobs. In certain positions, such as entry-level jobs and high-tech jobs, the labor situation will be even more critical.

The effort and investment required to hire, train, and develop top-performing employees is significant, and it dramatically impacts the bottom line. The more wages increase and the more jobs demand highly skilled workers, the more organizational effort it will take to fill those jobs. It is no wonder organizations are paying more attention to the acquisition and retention of their workforce.

Because of scarcity, cost, and impact of the workforce, many organizations are taking a significantly innovative approach to staffing. No longer is the staffing process within the organization separate or unconnected to its strategic business objectives. Executives now realize that just as getting customers, retaining customers, establishing product superiority, or creating marketplace dominance is important, having the organization staffed with capable, talented, and experienced individuals is of critical importance and should be a key strategic objective. Staffing is now considered a key element of the business strategy of many innovative organizations.

Changes in the Marketplace

For the first time, companies have begun acquiring other companies not for products, technology, customer base, or market share, but for their employees. The capability of employees can, in fact, be the most important asset considered in the decision to buy a given company.

Organizations that realize the importance of staffing also realize that they cannot reach their objectives by focusing on just one or two elements of the process. Attention cannot be placed solely on recruiting, for instance, ignoring the quality of hiring decisions. Retaining employees will reduce the need to hire, but unavoidable attrition and growth require continuous recruiting.

Progressive organizations are now approaching staffing in a holistic manner. Executives realize that hiring talented people is fruitless, unless employee needs are responded to, employees are rewarded for their efforts, and, like all precious assets, they are retained. Employers also realize that the quality of the individuals hired and the level of "fit" between the individuals and their particular jobs will determine the difficulty of the effort required to develop, reward, and retain them. Considering only one or two elements of this strategic objective alone is foolhardy because each is interrelated. One affects the other. The better one area is implemented, the easier the implementation of the others will become.

Implementing Holistic Staffing Methodology

If this innovative approach will increase success, the question you are probably asking is, "How can we do it in our organization?"

The first step in making any change is to declare its importance and the need for change to the company at large. For staffing to be strategic requires it to be identified as a business objective, and as such, elevated to the level of other critical organizational objectives. It doesn't do any good to make the "right" statements in company literature or distribute memos and e-mail declaring the importance of staffing, and yet spend time during staff meetings talking about sales, manufacturing, and service and only paying scant attention to questions such as, "How are we doing on getting our positions filled?"

By shifting the order and priority of staffing to the forefront, organizations can ensure they have staff who enable sales to be made, production levels to be hit, and customers to be satisfied. In short, to elevate staffing to a strategic level requires real, concrete action, not just lip service.

Shifting Priorities Successfully

In some organizations, shifting the priority of staffing to the forefront may require a change in mission, objectives, personnel, and even the structure of the Human Resources (HR) department. The HR department may have to be elevated in stature, resources, and even power. Human resources must take a more active role in strategic planning and key decision making.

Once the importance of staffing has been established and elevated to the strategic level, you can begin to improve hiring and staffing results. Begin by examining your current situation and identifying your needs. This examination can take the form of a staffing audit that analyze past actions such as employee intake, terminations, and their respective impacts.

In addition to simply reporting past statistics, other aspects of corporate history may come to light—such as the recruiting effort, hiring process, training and development, reward and recognition systems, and management of personnel. Experience has shown that employee attitude surveys are extremely enlightening. Organizations can create all the right reward and retention programs and say all the right things in their recruiting literature, but if the management does not reflect these values, it will all be wasted. In short, tremendous amounts of resources can be invested to create the right work environment and staff it with top performing individuals, only to have the actions of a few poorly trained or unenlightened managers erase the effort and cause significant turnover. Remember, with today's expanding job market and shrinking labor pool, employees have many positions to choose from and will not hesitate to move.

The Specifics of Planning

Organizations should develop a plan to ensure that objectives are met in each of their strategic areas. Staffing is no different. Begin developing the strategic plan to review your human capital by first assessing the organization's needs. Identify past turnover tendencies by tenure, job type, level, location, and other key factors to get a greater understanding of the causes. Examine exit interviews, executive interviews, and attitude surveys to determine the factors contributing to turnover.

Based on needs and financial factors such as salary levels and impact of loss, determine an acceptable turnover level by department and position. Evaluate the factors or reasons for turnover and determine the response or changes that must be made to bring turnover within the acceptable level. Keep in mind that while turnover can never be eliminated, it can be brought to a manageable level.

How Staffing and Planning Affect the Bottom Line

Recently, we conducted a turnover analysis for a division of a *Fortune 500* company. We found that if their turnover level for the past year had been reduced to the industry average, the savings would have equaled the dollar amount by which they missed their profit target. In short, if they had only reduced turnover to the industry average, they would have met the profit expectations for that division.

Experience has shown that for every dollar turnover costs are reduced, far more money actually goes to the bottom line, because turnover affects so many other areas of the organization's operation. The impact on customer retention may be difficult to calculate, but it is very tangible and substantial. Keeping good employees will help you keep good customers.

Looking Ahead

After you understand turnover, project the personnel needs for the organization, just as you would its financial needs for the future. Take into account factors such as overall business growth, replenishment for turnover, attrition due to factors such as termination and retirement, or movement of individuals to different jobs and locations.

Simply projecting needs, however, is not enough. With today's changing workforce it is important to define the knowledge and skills required for any given position or situation. The identification of need and the retraining of an employee to fit current needs is a critical part of any strategic approach. Utilizing and grooming current employees is a huge part of retention.

Now, more than ever, it is important to ensure that anyone

hired can be a top performing employee. As wages continue
to rise, increased productivity becomes an even more critical
factor to prevent inflation and reduced profits. One of the key
determinants of productivity is "job fit." Even highly motivated, intelligent, and skilled individuals will not be successful unless they have the natural attributes to match the work
they are being asked to accomplish.

To ensure those hired "fit" the position, first clearly define
each job. Identify the duties, responsibilities, level of performance, and career growth opportunities available. Then look
beyond the responsibilities and duties to determine the attributes of success. This visioning can be done by benchmarking
attributes of top performers. The resulting benchmarks may
be used to measure candidates' potential for performance.

Identifying Benchmarks

Some benchmarks or attributes are easier to identify than
others. In positions such as sales and management, for instance, the individual's behavior and values may be far more
important than his or her knowledge or skill. Identify or develop instruments or tools to assist in the selection of candidates to ensure they have the benchmarked attributes required. For example, if extroverted behavior is required for a
salesperson, being able to measure a candidate's personality
type allows for the determination of "job fit" between the individual and position. Most importantly, measuring "job fit"
makes possible better hiring decisions: employees who require less training and management and become higher performers faster.

How "Job Fit" Affects Turnover Rates

Recently, we found the most significant reason for turnover
for financial advisors at a Wall Street firm was poor "job fit,"
and we even isolated it to two primary attributes. It is important to note that the cost of their turnover to the company was
estimated at a minimum of $100,000 per financial advisor.

Knowing what attributes are necessary for a good "job fit" as a financial advisor and developing methods to measure presence of these attributes in a candidate would dramatically improve success and the bottom line. And, at $100,000 per successful identification, these factors become critical.

As business changes, it is important to periodically redefine the "job fit" for candidates. Once you know what you are looking for, develop the sources to ensure you have adequate candidate flow. By examining previous results, the best candidate sources can continuously be identified and your efforts focused on those sources.

It is important to continually look for new and innovative sources, as well. For example, several years ago the Internet may not have been a reliable source of non-technical candidates. However, this medium is improving daily and will only continue to gain in its importance and reliability. It is easy to think that one or two really good sources will meet all the staffing needs of a given company. However, as the labor pool shrinks and the competition for workers increases, it will be necessary to ensure that all sources are used to keep jobs filled. We can't afford to leave a source of good employees untapped.

Easing the Hiring Process

A well-designed and implemented selection process is necessary to ensure consistent results and to make hiring much easier. Identify the steps you will use, such as screening, interviewing, reference checking, background checking, hiring decision, and so forth. In the past, Human Resources departments have controlled and implemented the process. However, we now believe it is best to have those with a direct interest in the quality of the employee hired, such as line management, highly involved in the process. This involvement means that direct management personnel not only assist in the process, but also have ownership for those hired and a vested interest in their success. Monitoring and control by the HR department will help ensure the quality of the individual hired, the correct implementation of the process, and adherence to the legal requirements. Strive to achieve a partnership in the hiring process rather than a separation of departments.

The selection process should be monitored frequently to ensure that timetable and hiring objectives are being met. Tracking candidate flow and progress through the process helps spot problems and bottlenecks. Analysis can even determine the ratio or number of candidates needed for one hire. With this information, recruiting can be planned to ensure that positions will be filled by target dates. Applicant sources that have provided the greatest results can be identified and recruiting efforts can be focused on areas that provide the greatest return.

Continuously monitor turnover to identify problems. Don't just look at increases or problems. Look for positive changes and determine what works as well as what doesn't. Executive interviews, exit interviews, and most important, employee attitude surveys can help identify causes of existing turnover and predict future trends. Employee surveys identify levels of employee satisfaction, just as customer surveys determine levels of customer satisfaction and can point the way to improvements and the return on the effort to retain employees.

Treating the Staffing Process as Importantly as Your End Product

For years, organizations have monitored sales figures and customer satisfaction levels because they were two of the strategic elements of the organization's success. Employees, though, are the human capital, those who enable an organization to make a sale, produce a product, and serve a customer. You must allocate the same time, energy, and effort to monitor this element of your strategy as you would to monitor product quality control, cost management, or any other aspect of the bottom line. This human capital is the report card indicating your future success.

Whether your organization is high- or low-tech, public or private, small or large, it is only able to succeed because it is staffed with talented, motivated, capable employees. The quality and quantity of your staff is what your organization's success is built on. Build a firm foundation for your success by making the staffing process as important a process as any other in your company.

From Wayne Outlaw's chapter we gain an understanding of how to construct a solid foundation within your company to facilitate the best hiring decisions. In the coming chapter, Julie Moreland discusses the concept of job fit—that is, how well is any given employee suited for any specific job—to help employers learn how to best use existing employees and new hires. Moreland, president of an Atlanta consulting firm and an expert using assessment technologies, explores in detail how to change and supplement the hiring process in order to help you find the right employee for the right job

4

Selection
for Success

Julie Moreland, CMC

Selecting the Right Person
for the Right Job

Businesses have traditionally had two types of problems: *systems* problems and *people* problems. Systems problems are generally the easier of the two to solve. Systems issues are easier because they involve objective data that is usually quantifiable. Also, with systems, everyone is using a common frame of reference, with defined terminology and definitions. In other words, systems problems are, at the least, a known quantity.

With people problems, however, the situation is completely different; the data is almost always subjective. Descriptions of the same people problem can vary dramatically, depending on the point of view of the observer. Solutions are often based on strongly held opinions born of different circumstances with different people. These opinions, while valid for one person, frequently prove untenable when applied to another. People issues are further complicated by the emotions of the participants, which can mask or distort the facts. People problems, then, are rooted in a set of information that changes from situation to situation and from person to person.

It is managers' responsibility to find the solutions to both systems and people problems. Systems solutions may be relatively easily found, or at least may be found by an easily gained consensus. People problems, however, are more complicated. *All in all, an extraordinary amount of management time is spent each day trying to get smart, hard working employees to effectively and consistently perform the jobs that they were hired to do. We know why this happens. And now we know how to prevent it.*

Skills and Attitude

Job performance has always been understood through a two-part paradigm. An employee needed the right *skills* for the job, and that employee needed the right *attitude* for the job. The employee's attitude was a combination of the individual's values, ethics, and general outlook on life and work. His or her skills were thought to be a combination of the individual's experience, knowledge, and training. This paradigm is what determined management's response to unsatisfactory performance in the past.

If an employee appeared to have the right *attitude* and worked hard, then the problem appeared to be one involving a lack of skill. Consequently, management would utilize additional coaching and training to boost performance, and the problem was attributed to being a normal part of the learning curve. Sometimes this method was successful, and sometimes not.

Conversely, if a problem employee had the right *skills*, then the difficulty was considered to be one of attitude or motivation. Management would then turn to a variety of motivational strategies, ranging from offering bonuses to threatening dismissal. As with skill problems, the success of these solutions varied.

A Better Way

Over time, countless theories and methodologies were offered to explain or improve these results. Some suggested that better management techniques were needed, and better ones were developed. Still, success could not be adequately predicted or consistently achieved. Were some employees simply incompetent? Could some attitude problems not be solved? Motivational philosophies abounded, but the positive effects, when they occurred, were short-lived.

In response to these questions and more, several new personnel assessment instruments were developed in the 1990's specifically for use within the business world. It became possible to easily and accurately measure how people would behave in job situations and how they processed information. Moreover, it was discovered that the traits and abilities being measured by the new instruments were not trainable, coachable, or effectively changeable in any way. These traits were inherent in each individual.

Job Fit

These assessment systems were also designed to correlate data with job performance. The explosion of research revealed conclusively exactly how dependent job performance was on the employee's core personality traits and cognitive abilities. When this third component of job performance—*job fit*—was combined with the other components, attitude and skills, the cornerstones were complete.

When job fit was understood, it was easy to see why some people struggled in certain positions after being successful in others. It was easy to see why smart people, working hard, still failed in certain jobs. And it was possible to see why even well-designed training, motivation, and coaching were often not successful. Employers had to find the right person for the right job.

Skills and attitude were as important as always, but the notion of job fit opened the door to countless new opportunities for managers and business owners. Attitude could be influenced with management style and the working environment. Skills could definitely be learned, and experience could be acquired. It was job fit, however, that tended to remain the same despite coaching, training, and various incentives.

Armed with this knowledge and understanding, managers could now focus on developing positions that took advantage of each individual's particular strengths. Training programs could focus on skills and knowledge issues rather than questionable performance problem solving. Managers could understand from the first day how best to direct a new employee with the kind of information the new assessments provided. The findings challenged many classic career path assumptions by showing how moving from one job to another often demanded dramatically different core behaviors, sometimes even opposite extremes of behavior. It even explained classic promotion conundrums such as the top salesperson who on promotion, fails as a sales manager.

How Job Fit Changed the Workplace

Selection and recruiting techniques were forever changed. The most effective interviewing techniques of the top interviewing professionals could not match the results of average managers using the new technologies. Several of the newest assessment tools even provided behavioral event-based interview questions that could be matched to the behavioral profile of the individual candidates and the job. This provision of questions enabled managers to conduct focused and effective interviews without extensive training. It also tended to standardize the interview process across a diverse range of interviewers with varying skill levels. In other words, it became possible, in a somewhat scientific manner, to find the right person for the job. An added benefit from these systems was that it became easier to achieve objective and nondiscriminatory hiring practices in compliance with current legal regulations.

The biggest challenge for businesses seeking to use these new hiring technologies is how to fit them into existing hiring programs. After all, even the best and most effective technologies are useless if incompletely understood or incorrectly used. While different businesses of course have different situations with different components, it is possible to offer practical suggestions and general guidelines for implementing more effective hiring and promotion strategies.

Some Basic Rules and Guidelines for Effective Selection Systems

1. Remember that you cannot train your way out of a bad hiring decision.
2. The cost of hiring one poor employee is far greater than the cost of having an effective selection process.
3. Using new assessment technology by itself will avoid poor hires more dependably than the most extensive interviews by the most talented interviewers using the best techniques for interviewing.
4. Assessments will dependably screen out people who cannot do the job.
5. Assessments do not, however, dependably point out star performers. The good news is that you can still make money with average employees in a well-run business. It is the poor performers that destroy profits.
6. Use the least expensive and most accurate screening method first. For example, if a ten-minute assessment that costs $10 will screen out poor performers, do that before spending valuable interview time with someone who is unlikely to be able to succeed at the job anyway.
7. Use drug testing if employees interact with customers,

use machinery, use tools, or drive vehicles on company business.

8. Use background checks if employees handle money, interact with customers, or drive vehicles on company business.
9. Use honesty/integrity testing if employees handle money or valuable tools and material.
10. Consult with a labor law attorney who represents management when you have any doubts or questions.

Basic Selection System Components

A basic selection system that could be used in most businesses consists of an initial quick screen; a brief interview; a quick job match assessment; drug/integrity testing; and behavioral event-based or structured interviews.

Initial Quick Screen

This process can be performed by reviewing solicited résumés, by telephone, or by e-mail. If the job requires a particular certification, a particular amount of experience, a particular preexisting skill, a particular schedule, definite degrees of flexibility, specific travel demands, particular transportation, or something else that is essential and specific, confirm that the candidate meets that qualification before spending any more time or money.

Brief Interview

This interview is a five- to 15-minute face-to-face greeting. After obtaining the necessary application paperwork from a high volume of candidates, administrative staff should conduct a brief interview. For more select positions, the interview would be done by the initial decision-maker for the hiring. This person might be the owner of a small business, a member of management in a large company, or anyone in between. The purpose of this brief meeting is simply to verify that the candidate's initial attitude, grooming, and verbal skills are acceptable for the existing job standards. Specific experience can be explored, but in-depth questions should be reserved for later interviews.

Quick Job Match Assessment

If the brief interview is satisfactory, the next step is for the candidate to complete a quick survey to evaluate the best job fit. There are several assessment products on the market that require about ten minutes, cost about $10–$15, and accurately measure core behavioral traits relative to various jobs. They also measure cognitive ability or reasoning speed. By using these tools, candidates who are a poor match for certain jobs can be directed into other areas.

Special Note: One important application of these instruments is in the pre-screening of out-of-town candidates. The personality section of the assessments can determine if the job fit is sufficient to warrant the usually high expense of bringing a candidate into town for interviews.

Drug Testing/Integrity Testing

If appropriate for the job in question, drug/integrity tests should be performed at this point. These tests are usually the next least expensive and most accurate part of the process. Also, since a positive drug test or a poor score on an honesty/integrity test will usually cause an exit from the candidate pool, expensive interview time should not be invested until those issues are settled. Integrity testing normally requires 15–20 minutes and costs $15–$20. Drug testing varies according to the type of test. There are multiple options that allow for quick results while a candidate is on-site. If necessary, more detailed results can be acquired, after conditional job offers are made.

Special Note: Currently, many companies are faced with low unemployment rates and strong competition for skilled workers. Often they are challenged to find enough candidates to even fill the open positions, and the concept of screening out any of them is not acceptable. The liabilities posed by employees who fail to meet minimal standards are potentially huge. *It is important to temper the urgent need to fill positions with conservative caution in order to protect the overall business.*

Behavioral Event-Based Interviews or Structured Interviews

At this point in the process, the focus changes from screening out unsatisfactory candidates to selecting the best candidate from those that remain. If few candidates are available, this process focuses on understanding how best to use the employees who will be hired. This approach includes understanding how to compensate for those behaviors that may not match the demands of the job.

Interviews should always be planned in advance. The newest screening assessments provide interview questions that are tailored to each candidate and to the job. This tailoring saves the interviewer from having to prepare questions and standardizes the process for each candidate. Behavioral event-based interview questions are generally the most effective in collecting information about the candidate's past experience. This method requires the candidate to relate actual events from previous situations as examples of certain behaviors, a method much more effective than traditional questions that explore feelings and attitudes and ask the candidate to speculate on future behavior in hypothetical situations.

Now What? Putting It All Together

A simple yet effective way of putting all of the information together is to use the three-part paradigm of attitude, skills, and job fit. Some form of numerical rating scale can be used to rate each candidate in terms of satisfying the requirements of the job in each of these categories. Sub-categories can be developed to simplify this process, such as breaking the attitude component into separate categories: energy level, enthusiasm, grooming, verbal skills, knowledge of the company, and so forth. Rating scales have the advantage of creating a relative ranking of candidates for the same job. The rankings are certainly subjective in many ways, but these subjective rankings still allow for the process to be objectified as much as possible at the decision point. Some assessments provide forms for this ranking as a part of their systems.

Additional Steps

Depending on the nature of the position being filled, it may be desirable to obtain a deeper level of information about candidates for key jobs. More information may be needed because the jobs are at a high level; because they have high salaries; because they involve complex responsibilities; or because they are critical to the profitable operation of the business. The recommended procedure for candidates at this point is to administer a more sophisticated assessment instrument that is designed for this purpose.

These kinds of instruments have detailed cognitive scales of measurement, which can reveal the candidate's ability to think strategically, tactically, and creatively, to solve problems quickly, to express ideas at an executive level, to deal with abstract concepts, to visualize data flows and more. These assessments also measure personality traits in great detail, and they produce a level of information that can project almost any kind of work behavior. They can also be used to engineer team interactions.

Once this assessment information is available, you should conduct an in-depth interview. The focus now centers on how the candidate's various talents, abilities, experience, and behavioral competencies can be used within the company. It should also be the forum for exploring the candidate's own understanding of personal weaknesses and how those weaknesses could be handled constructively in the position in question.

This selection process is, of course, a general recommendation. Each company should consider its own particular needs and its own situation when devising its selection process. It may be important to secure the advice of professionals when necessary.

Keep in mind that there will never be one true and foolproof method for selecting the right employees. However, the selection process described above can put you closer to finding that perfect fit than ever before.

For More Information

Internet users can visit http://careers.altavista.com/emp/russell.html and in five minutes can get an evaluation of their hiring practices. The report identifies potential liabilities, inefficiencies, diseconomies, and opportunities. It also recommends corrective actions, all at no cost.

Read *Right Person—Right Job, Guess or Know* by Chuck Russell, a quick primer on the new strategies of selecting with assessment tools.

As Julie Moreland points out, there will never be one foolproof method for finding the right employees. However, just as she sought to do in her chapter, the next chapter, by her partner Chuck Russell, seeks to make the process as foolproof as possible. Russell, the senior partner of Jobfun.com, has been a leader in the area of differentiating elastic and non-elastic tendencies that determine performance of employees and within employee groups. His chapter details the uses and the power of assessment technology in today's workforce. He discusses ways of best implementing these exciting new technologies and provides key elements to look for in any assessment product.

5

Selection Tools and Their Applications

Chuck Russell

The Power of Assessment Technology

Imagine a business that competes in your industry. Imagine that this business made a simple change in the way it hired and managed its employees. Imagine that because of this simple change, the business never again hired the wrong person for a key job. Furthermore, by matching the right people to the right jobs, productivity for this business jumped 20 percent or more. Imagine that because of this simple change, the time needed to make a risk-free hiring decision collapsed to several hours, instead of days or weeks.

Thus in a low unemployment market with everyone competing for good workers, this business has a considerable recruiting advantage in capturing top candidates. Imagine that this simple change results in a significant reduction in hiring expenses, in addition to driving a more efficient process. Imagine that this simple change costs about the same as providing coffee for employees, requires only minimal training, and can work within whatever procedures or systems are already in place.

How would you compete with this business? Can you spot your competitors a 20 percent advantage in productivity? If they can hire the better candidates more quickly and more cheaply than you can, where will you find workers? Who will be left for your key hires? These are all critical questions that have been thrust into the spotlight because of the advent of performance information technology.

Performance information technology refers to the vast array of products, processes, systems, and methodologies that are designed to evaluate how well an individual will perform in a particular job and apply that information to recruiting, selection, hiring, management, and training. The concept is quite old and has had a somewhat checkered history. However, with the easy availability of high-speed computers, the growth of an information economy, and the development of more reliable means of measurement, the right tools became available to take serious research into the practical world of business.

How Selection Technology Began

Some of the best minds in psychology partnered with some of the most effective performance management specialists and began to seek ways in which to create more effective performance information indicators. They began to focus their attention on understanding the critical factors of job performance. The success of this quest was made more important by today's intensely competitive business environment, the globalization of competition through the Internet, and the increasing challenge of finding suitable employees.

It has long been known that people have certain core personality traits that tend to remain stable. These traits form the foundation of every person's strengths and weaknesses, and they can be accurately measured. By comparing an individual's traits to the behaviors needed in a particular job, it is easy to see which ones will serve as strengths in a given job and which ones will be weaknesses in that job.

The most important finding of the latest research has been that the core traits of any individual are only good or bad relative to a specific job. In other words, everyone is good for some jobs, but no one is good for all jobs. Everyone is bad for some jobs; no one is bad for all jobs. This finding means that the value of an employee can be determined by how well the company matches an employee to the right job.

The Potential in the Marketplace

The promise of this discovery is extraordinary. It has the potential to transform virtually every aspect of human resources, performance management, and training. The catch (and you knew there must be one) is that these simple and effective tools can be incredibly difficult to find. The marketplace is awash with nearly 80,000 occupational-related assessments, hundreds of interviewing systems, and countless other methodologies. To make matters worse, each of these assessments is usually sold by a salesperson dedicated to that product and that methodology. Therefore, the most interested and diligent buyer generally has incomplete information on a very small part of the available spectrum, presented by a biased source. Even psychologists, whose practices are focused on business issues, are seldom up to date on the most current advances in assessment technology.

In fact, the odds are against the average business executive discovering one of the handful of truly revolutionary products. The vast quantity of assessments found in the marketplace are relics from the theories of the 1940's, 1950's, and 1960's. Although these assessments were printed yesterday and boast the latest buzzwords, their underlying thinking has long been abandoned by the serious thinkers of today. We're not saying that such products have no value. Virtually all assessments provide some level of information that may be valuable. The inescapable truth, however, is that this information is simply not comparable to what is possible with modern tools, any more than the original electronic game, Pong, could challenge the Sony Play Station or Nintendo in terms of entertainment value.

The appearance of most performance information testing systems is similar. Each set of information, whether it is the output of the newest product or the oldest one, contains *some* accurate information. This information can be deceiving to the buyer, since the "Try one and see what you think" will almost always result in a positive impression. Unfortunately, it is the information that is missing from the older tests that is dangerous. Newer products offer a much greater depth of behavioral definition that can make a serious difference in critical business decisions. Newer products also include a type of "lie detector" scale that helps to identify those candidates who may try to "fool the test."

Further complicating the issue is the fact that many of these systems were developed initially for the purpose of pre-employment screening of job applicants. For most companies today, the first priority is finding enough candidates to fill their open positions. The idea of reducing that number by some form of screening seems counterproductive.

Though the recruiting environment is increasingly smaller in today's marketplace, information generated by the latest tools can dramatically aid recruiting efforts. First of all, by shrinking the time required to make a reasonably risk-free decision, new technologies enable smart companies to capture top-level candidates who previously were lost to competitors with a faster selection process. Second, by defining the specific performance issues of marginal candidates, smart companies are able to place them in positions with minimal exposure. Third, by identifying highly qualified potential candidates immediately, career paths can be more effectively planned and used during the recruiting process.

The Bottom Line Strength of Assessment Technology

The power of the newest assessment technology to provide information that both accelerates decision making while at the same time minimizes the risk of those decisions is exciting for any executive in a competitive business. It is thrilling to imagine the opportunities and possibilities described in the beginning of this chapter being those of your own company, and not those of your competition. Consider these questions:

- What would be possible in your company if no one was ever put in the wrong job?
- If you could see exactly how existing employees are mismatched to their current jobs so that you could fix it, would you?
- If productivity in your company increased by 20 percent, what would be the most immediate changes? What would happen to your market share?
- If you could pinpoint training issues for each individual and sort them into what could be trained and what could not, how would you spend your training budget differently?
- If you could make risk-free job offers within 24 hours, how would it affect your recruiting?

Imagine you have traveled back in time, back to when you first heard about what computers or the Internet would mean to businesses. You have just read about something that will revolutionize the people part of business to the same extent. Performance information technology is the next wave that is going to bring sweeping change to the business world. Act now and explore the possibilities. Don't be left behind.

For More Information

- Read a book called *Right Person-Right Job, Guess or Know*, a one-hour read filled with practical ideas.
- Try out some of the newer assessments. Contact The Workforce Stability Institute for some suggestions and sample case studies.
- Visit www.rightperson-rightjob.com. You can read about various tests and even request reviews and opinions directly from the site. You cannot buy tests there, but there are links to many different assessment sites.

Once you have the right assessment technology in place, it's time to explore new and innovative ways of finding employees. It's no longer enough just to hang a "Help Wanted" sign in your window. Everyone has already done that. In today's ultra-competitive employee market, you must differentiate yourself from your competition. In short, you must market your company to prospective hires. Catherine Fyock, a longtime seminar leader, seasoned speaker, and expert on training and development, writes about the notion of branding your company just as you would a product; she develops the idea of selling your company to employees on the market or even in other jobs as the best place to work.

6

Recruiting the Best

Catherine D. Fyock, CSP, SPHR

Recruiting Today's Elusive Job Candidate

With unemployment rates reaching record lows, most of today's viable job candidates are already employed elsewhere. The challenge for recruiters seeking the best candidates, then, is how to reach those people who are not even looking for a job.

The problem with most traditional recruitment tactics is that they are designed with active job seekers in mind. For example, if your organization places a recruitment advertisement in the Help Wanted section of the newspaper, you are making an assumption that the candidates you want are seeking employment and looking in this section of the paper.

But how can employers attract those candidates already employed in other capacities, those candidates who skip right through the want ads? What are the strategies that employers can use to attract these elusive job seekers cost-effectively?

The concepts and ideas detailed below should improve your recruitment results.

Selling What You Have to Offer

Most candidates who are happily employed elsewhere will need to be "sold" on the idea of working with your organization. Therefore, you cannot merely list the job requirements in your advertisements; you need to "woo" candidates by spelling out what's in it for them. Focus on the benefits and advantages of working in your organization in language they can understand. Conduct focus groups with current employees to determine the best selling factors to emphasize in your advertisements.

You'll also need to create compelling advertisements that grab the attention of those readers, even those not looking for a job. Place eye-catching ads in other sections of the newspaper such as the television, sports, or food sections. Bold graphics, use of color, illustrations, pictures, and catchy headlines are other ways to capture the attention of that elusive candidate.

Remember: you're selling a product, just as any other advertisement is. In this case, though, you're selling yourself and your company.

Offer Response Options

Traditionally, employers have limited access to their employment offices in an attempt to maintain efficiency. For example, one client had a sign posted on their employment office door indicating that they only accepted applications on Tuesdays and Thursdays, within certain time periods. What they failed to recognize is that while they increased the efficiency of the employment office by using this technique, they also reduced the applications received from good candidates who were employed elsewhere and could not be accommodated by the two-day schedule.

Today's employers will need to provide new and varied response options to attract candidates who are working else-where. Consider the following:

- A clip-out coupon that can be mailed or faxed
- A 24-hour telephone line that enables candidates to call any time the day that the advertisement appears
- Evening and weekend employment office hours

Remember, also, that if you require a résumé as the first step in your employment process, you may be excluding those who are too busy in their current jobs to respond.

Using Intrusive Techniques

Intrusive recruitment techniques assume the right candidate is working someplace else. Third-party recruitment is an ex-cellent example of intrusive recruitment. Candidates are con-tacted directly by phone to determine if they or someone they know is interested in a specific opportunity. While third-party recruiters can do an exceptional job in identifying top candidates, the costs may be high. Many employers are seek-ing lower cost options that can yield the same successful re-sults. To accomplish this goal of keeping costs low and meth-ods in-house, employers use intrusive techniques such as telemarketing, direct mail, and employee referral.

Telemarketing is essentially doing in-house what recruit-ment firms have done for years. Employers obtain the tele-phone numbers of potential candidates by purchasing a list from research companies, through databases, or from re-cruitment advertising agencies. Alternatively, some organi-zations use free telephone listings from school rosters, pro-fessional directories, and the like. Then, the employer con-tacts these candidates directly to determine if the candidate is interested in opportunities with the firm.

Direct mail is increasingly used for intrusive recruit-ment. Again, mailing lists can be obtained by contacting professional organizations, publications, seminar companies, research companies, and recruitment advertising agencies.

Focus your list by specifying certain types of backgrounds or criteria, such as:

- Position title
- Industry/SIC code
- Zip code/city/state/region

Tailor the mailing to your audience, and increase response rates by offering varied response options. A personal appeal—a mailing that looks like a letter or invitation—is generally more effective than a commercial approach—a brochure or slick advertising piece.

Employee referral is yet another intrusive strategy that targets those already employed. Ask new employees during their orientation to provide you with the names and contact information of three to five people they might recommend from their last job, or those they know from school, church, or social activities. Don't wait for the employee to make contact—act on this information immediately by making the call yourself, using the employee's name as a means to establish a "warm" lead.

Finding Top Candidates

Given the increasing difficulty of finding and attracting top candidates, the changing and competitive labor market, and evolving worker demographics, employers must develop more creative strategies to recruit top candidates. The remainder of this chapter outlines new recruitment ideas that will assist organizations in rethinking ways to creatively attract the best candidates.

Talent Scout Cards

One ingenious retailer in search of sales associates printed "talent scout" cards—just a little bigger than a business card— to give out to workers demonstrating customer service skills within the community. When a manager observed an exceptionally friendly, service-oriented individual (at the grocery store, restaurant, dry cleaners, or wherever), the manager would provide a talent scout card indicating the company's need for service-minded employees. The card discussed the opportunities that the retailer had for its employees and included a toll-free number to call for information.

Point of Sale Messaging

If customers are a potential source of qualified employees, then consider using point of sale recruitment messages—especially for retailers and others with direct customer contact. Use point of purchase brochures, a counter card, or even cash register receipts to relay the message. Messages should be positive, however, so that the implication of offering less quality service is avoided. One business used the message, "Place your name on our employment waiting list for great job opportunities." Even though this employer didn't have a "waiting list" at the time, the employer was able to create one once the word was out. An employer with a waiting list is perceived as an excellent place to work.

Layoffs/Closings

When other businesses in the community close or lay off employees, there may be a great chance to recruit top-notch, experienced candidates. Watch the newspaper for information on these business opportunities, keep in touch with local professional human resources organizations, or call the local chamber of commerce.

Posters

Posters placed in the community can be a low-cost, effective way to appeal to job candidates. Place posters in community centers, churches, grocery stores, pharmacies, laundromats, banks, and other locations where there are community bulletin boards. Posters can be made at a local quick print shop for those recruiters operating with "no budget" budgets. Consider using a tear-off "mini-application" form (which can also be made at the quick print shop), so candidates will be able to easily respond. Include contact information, as well as a code, so that the most effective posters and locations can be determined.

Door Hangers

Placing recruitment messages door-to-door can be another low-cost, yet effective way to reach potential job candidates within a specific geographic area.

Bargain Shoppers

Whether they're called the *Penny Pincher*, the *Thrifty Nickel*, or the *Bargain Mart* in your community, bargain shopper newspapers can be an effective, low-cost medium for advertising entry-level and hourly job openings.

Radio

Consider the use of public service announcements (PSAs) to advertise job openings at no cost. Pay for radio advertising when a specific listener audience is being targeted—each radio station can provide their listener demographics. Radio is best used when print advertising accompanies and reinforces the audio message. For example, to advertise for an open house event, refer radio listeners to a print message (in Sunday's paper, perhaps) that provides all the details for the event. As in any advertising venue, make sure that the demographics match your needs.

Television

Cable television bulletin board channels may offer some low-cost methods to place recruitment messages. Moreover, many stations offer public service announcements for job openings that cost the employer nothing.

Billboards

Today, recruitment messages are even beginning to work

their way onto highway billboard signs, electronic billboards at sports events, and portable billboards that can be rented for a modest amount. Use concise language, and be positive in the message that is chosen. The best billboard messaging is short and clear, and is often 15 words or less. Make it easy for your audience to remember your message.

Sign-on Bonuses

Many industries, most notably health care, have been offering sign-on bonuses for years. A sign-on bonus is a flat dollar amount that is given to new employees when they begin work. Some organizations use a waiting period before the bonus is paid to discourage those who are "job-hopping" just to get a bonus. Sign-on bonuses work best when they are unique to the industry or to the geographic area.

"New" Recruitment Agencies

Just a few years ago, agencies could only be used for upper management and professional and technical positions because of the high cost. However, today there are many new breeds of agencies that are working to find top-notch job candidates for all levels within the organization. Seek agencies that offer very low fee rates (often lower than 20 percent of the new employee's starting annual salary), or that charge by the hour for the search. Negotiate with agencies for the best package of services. Some agencies are providing research services only; others offer videotaping of top job candidates in various geographic locations. Be sure to check references when using any new service.

Employment "Hotline"

Making it easy for the job candidate to reach employers is fast becoming an essential ingredient of a successful recruitment strategy, especially when the ideal job candidate is most likely currently working elsewhere. One low-cost method employers can use that enables candidates to explore the current position offerings is an employment "hotline." The employer merely adds a dedicated line with a recorded message answering machine, which changes as the employment opportunities change within the organization. In this way, potential applicants can call in at their convenience—often not during "regular" employment office hours.

Employers are also beginning to answer their telephones on Sunday to entice those who are browsing in the newspaper to explore opportunities when it is convenient for job seekers.

1-800 Numbers

Employers are increasingly adding 800 numbers to facilitate out-of-town candidates' opportunity to explore job opportunities. Employers can either manage this option in-house or can contract with recruitment advertising agencies and third-party providers to offer this service. Generally, the cost of these services is based on telephone inquiry volume, the number of questions candidates are to be asked, and other variables.

Alternate Sections of the Newspaper

Try advertising in alternate sections of the newspaper—not the "Help Wanted" and classified sections—to attract candidates who are not actively seeking employment. Consider the candidates you want to attract, and place ads in the sections with high readership of those labor market segments. For example, women may be attracted by ads appearing in the grocery store section on coupon days; older adults may see ads where they are looking each day—the television section, food section, and even the obituary section. Use clip-out coupon type ads that enable candidates without current résumés to explore job options immediately.

Marketing/Public Relations Department Partnerships

Human resource professionals seeking to enhance their organization's image as a good employer may want to team up with their marketing and public relations departments. Marketing professionals can share information on marketing campaigns; public relations executives can assist in developing press releases and other media contacts to enhance the employment image. Often, these departments have budgets that can be shared with human resources to achieve mutual goals.

Information Seminars

When candidates no longer are attracted to open houses or career fairs, one alternative method is to conduct an information seminar in which the hosting employer engages a speaker to discuss a topic of importance to potential job candidates. For example, one food service employer hosted a "career search" seminar on topics such as résumé preparation, job search strategies, interviewing techniques, and follow-up methods. At the end of the presentation, the employer provided a "commercial" about career opportunities and scheduled one-on-one appointments with those candidates who wanted to discuss the employer's opportunities. This employer had been trying, without success, to recruit candidates through traditional open houses. By using this new approach, both the quality and the quantity of candidates improved.

In Atlanta, a major department store and a temporary help agency joined forces to provide career search seminars, and ended up attracting many more candidates who were interested in re-entering the job market than had been attracted through more traditional means.

One company in search of information systems professionals sponsored a seminar featuring state-of-the-art technologies relating to that profession. Not only was the event successful in attracting job candidates who were dedicated to staying on top of the industry, but the employer was also able to make it comfortable for potential job seekers to attend the event without feeling that they were committing to a job.

Welcome Wagon and Realtors®

Why not attract those who are relocating to the community by working closely with those organizations whose business it is to either relocate or welcome those moving? Many businesses have developed successful partnerships with Welcome Wagon or newcomers organizations to identify potential community newcomers who are looking for employment opportunities.

Realtors®, especially those with corporate relocation departments, are increasingly offering career assistance for relocating spouses and family members. Develop relationships with these Realtors®, and offer job search assistance and counseling to families who are relocating to the community.

Acting While You Can

In today's tight labor market, we must use different strategies to attract that elusive job seeker—the person happily and successfully employed elsewhere. Only then can organizations get the best employees to meet their staffing goals. The same marketing strategies used to sell products, from shoes to shower caps, can be used to sell your product: your company. Remember that your marketplace is every bit as competitive as any sales environment, and act accordingly.

We turn from self-marketing back to Wayne Outlaw for a discussion of the nuts and bolts of the hiring process. After all, once you've promoted your company to employees, they still have to make the grade. Outlaw guides readers though the ABCs of the hiring process and suggests ways of humanizing what often can be a grueling system. He also provides advice for how best to implement the interview process from start to hiring. His comprehensive look at hiring and staffing presents some interesting ideas and updates some tried and true methods.

7

Performance-Based Interviews

Wayne Outlaw, CSP, CMC

Uncovering Past Performance to Predict Future Performance

The interview is not only the greatest tool available to help you select the right candidate, it also is the time in the employment process when you are the most vulnerable and legally exposed.

Even if you do a great job in all other aspects of hiring, your effort will be wasted unless you use effective interviewing techniques and invest the time and effort to conduct thorough, in-depth interviews. How well you and your staff perform during these meetings will greatly determine your ability to select a top person who can make a significant contribution and increase the success of the organization.

While people do change, the best indication of future performance is the individual's past performance. The behavior displayed in previous positions is, unless something dramatic has occurred, likely to be repeated in the next position. While many managers are optimistic and feel that people change, don't expect change just because the employee is in a new position, unless there is discernible evidence of change.

Because people's behavior in similar situations is usually consistent, selection of employees for positions should be based on discovering past performance and comparing it to the requirements of the job(s) for which they are being considered. If, during the interview, examples of the types of behavior required to be successful in the new job are consistently uncovered, it is likely that that behavior will be exhibited in the new job.

This chapter will suggest means for conducting an effective and thorough interview. By learning these techniques and putting them into practice, you can enhance your ability to identify candidates who have a very high probability of success and long-term retention.

Begin your preparation for a performance-based interview by ensuring that you know the criteria for performance in the position. You will use this preparation to evaluate the candidate's potential for being a top performer. The questions asked and the information gathered will enable you to evaluate the candidate against the hiring criteria you have established and the qualifications of other candidates. The hiring criteria are determined by defining the job responsibilities, duties, expected level of performance, and career growth potential. Use the attitudes, values, and capabilities a candidate *must* have to successfully perform the job as the benchmark. Examine how well the candidate displayed these qualities in previous positions.

Because past performance is the most reliable indicator of future performance, it is only logical that we carefully examine past performance in similar positions and situations. In consulting situations, we have used our proprietary

"Performance-based Selection Techniques" to assist clients in making informed hiring decisions.

Interview Objectives

The primary objectives during the interview are to determine if the candidate will be a top-performing individual, will fit into the organization, and will have a high probability of staying with the company. Your questions should focus on the individual's past performance, especially in areas that relate to the position. Carefully examine the candidate's behavior. Far too many interviewers ask about the future. They ask the candidate "what-if" questions that do not accurately predict future behavior. Many people can describe something they can or want to do. By focusing heavily on previous job performance and how it was accomplished, you easily obtain information that can be verified during reference and background checks. With this detailed and specific information, you can determine if the candidate was a high-performer or is simply a highly persuasive candidate.

Styles of Interviews

Over the years, several different interview styles have been developed that fit specific needs. No one style is perfect; each style addresses different needs. Too much emphasis or reliance should not be placed on any one technique or interview style.

Serial Interviews

The serial interview builds on previous interviews; each subsequent interview provides more detailed and in-depth information. Information obtained during the interview is compiled on an interview evaluation form and it, along with any concerns, questions, and additional areas to be probed, are passed to the next interviewer. The evaluation form allows the next interviewer to prepare for the subsequent interview by determining the specific areas to be examined. Questions can be preplanned.

Serial style interviews connect subsequent interviews to each other and create a progression of more in-depth and meaningful evaluations. Even if interviewers use this style, there is no specific mention of this to the candidate. The candidate probably perceives interviewers as being very astute or assumes the interviewers have spoken with each other. The candidate should not be "grilled" about what was said in previous interviews; an interrogation environment must not evolve.

Serial style interviews require a short period of time between interviews to allow for completion of the evaluation and preparation by the next interviewer. The time can be as short as a few minutes, but the candidate cannot go directly from one interview into the next.

Patterned Interviews

Many interviewers are ineffective because they have no structure or consistency to their interview and simply begin asking questions. Effective interviews are structured. The objective of this style of interview is to make sure all important areas are covered. It may be as simple as pre-planning several questions on each of the *musts* in the hiring criteria for all candidates. Each interview should include consistent questions on the position and performance in previous positions.

Some companies put great stock in this type of interview and the structure may be elaborate and detailed. With positions in sales, customer service, and management, where interpersonal skills are critical, the pattern style interview can be especially effective. With a pre-planned list in hand, the interviewer asks predictive, revealing questions that provide solid information to make a hiring decision. Because of the need to obtain a great deal of information quickly and easily for comparison with other applicants, most screening interviews follow this style.

Written Interviews

To reduce the administrative burden of interviewing, some organizations have created written interviews. Well thought out and prepared written questions, primarily about the candidate's experience and interest, reveal a great deal. Many questions have pre-determined acceptable responses to assist in screening out non-candidates.

Because the applicant must respond in writing, this style can be especially beneficial if a large part of the job consists of written communication. It allows a larger number of candidates to be interviewed in a shorter time because it eliminates the time requirement for one-to-one communication.

Panel Interviews

This style of interview involves multiple interviewers in one session, who ask a candidate prepared questions. The panel is usually made up of three or more persons from upper management or even outside resources, such as consultants. It can give those involved in a hiring decision the same opportunity to see and hear the candidate's response. This style has a fairly rigid format and tends to limit probing doubtful areas with follow-up questions.

The major drawback to this style is that it can be stressful, and if continued for very long, it can be grueling for the candidate. The candidate may get the impression he or she is being "ganged-up" on. History has not shown a clear correlation between the ability to do well in a panel style interview and future success.

This style of interview tends to be used by larger corporations and academic institutions when a candidate is being evaluated for entrance into a specific program such as a management development or an advanced degree.

Types of Interviews

There are three common types of interviews that are used for very distinct and different purposes. The interviewer must keep in mind the purpose when planning and carrying out interviews.

Screening Interviews

Screening interviews are effective in obtaining information to determine if the individual is a viable candidate. They are not designed to determine whether to hire the person, but simply to determine if the applicant meets the *musts*. The length of a screening interview is usually fifteen to thirty minutes and may be done on the phone or in person. Using the phone is a very productive way to screen a large number of applicants quickly. Only their applications or résumés and responses are considered to determine candidacy, and judgment tends to be more objective and performance-based.

Screening interviews usually consist of specifically prepared questions for all applicants and questions developed from the applicant's background. Screening interviews are the type conducted on campus and at events like job fairs or open houses.

In-depth Interviews

This type of interview is designed to uncover more in-depth information about someone who is deemed a candidate. The length of an in-depth interview is from forty-five minutes to one and one-quarter hours. It usually takes more than forty-five minutes for the interviewer to relax the candidate and get the in-depth information needed to make a decision. When interviews are longer than one and one-quarter hour, questions tend to become redundant, fatigue becomes a factor, and effectiveness diminishes as the interview continues.

It is a good idea to get a second opinion before making any important decision, and hiring is no different. It is best to have at least two in-depth interviews conducted by different managers. The advantage of multiple interviewers is there will be multiple evaluations that can be compared. Questions or unresolved concerns from one interview can be followed up by the next. Linking in-depth interviews by different managers during a short period of time creates a serial style interview, which is an excellent way to check for consistency of responses.

It is also good to schedule interviews on multiple days because they provide more information than a single impression. Many mistakes can be avoided by asking the candidate to come back for a subsequent interview. Having a second interview, even if it has to be done by the same interviewer at a later time, is critical.

Buy-off Interviews

Upper management uses buy-off interviews to confirm decisions made by the hiring manager. Buy-off interviews are only conducted with candidates who have been selected for hiring. These interviews generally occur after all reference and background checks have been performed. They are usually the last step before extending offers. Buy-off interviews allow confirmation that the hiring process is being implemented properly, that the individuals meet or exceed company standards, and that the managers have made good hiring decisions. All worksheets and pre-employment evaluations should be completed and available for review prior to the buy-off interviews. Normally, the persons conducting buy-off interviews check to ensure the quality of the hiring process and decisions. It is not necessary to inform candidates that these are buy-off interviews or that they are the last steps because it could create the expectation of an imminent job offer.

The level of involvement by upper management will vary depending on the hiring manager's skill and track record. It can be a full-length interview similar to an in-depth interview or a short chat, by phone or in person. When the hiring manager has a proven track record, the buy-off interview may simply be a review of the candidate's file to validate the manager's decision. This conference is a good opportunity to coach the hiring manager and assist him or her in improving hiring skills.

Preparation

The time spent preparing for an interview is critical. First, consider the time and place of the interview. Schedule it at a convenient time and place for the manager and the applicant. Be sure there is ample time and the site is quiet, private, comfortable, and free from distractions.

Next, review the application or résumé and compare the findings to the performance criteria of the position the candidate is interested in. Take the time to develop prepared questions that probe any red flags or other specific concerns.

Even the most skilled interviewer will benefit by preparing a list of questions in advance. Many untrained interviewers go on fishing expeditions because they feel prepared questions limit them. This fishing expedition style can produce bizarre questions that have no relationship to job performance and detract from the effectiveness of the interview.

Have the proper forms ready and notepads handy for temporary notes during the interview. *Do not write on the job application.* It is a document provided to the company in pursuit of employment. Take temporary notes that can later be consulted or even discarded, so you can accurately complete an interview evaluation.

Structure of In-depth Interviews

The most effective interviews have structure but are not rigid. They are structured enough to cover all areas and flexible enough to allow the interviewer to probe any areas of concern or red flags and follow through on the candidate's responses. The following is a thumbnail guide to interview structure.

Introduction

The purpose of the introduction is to relax the applicant and promote open, candid communication. Begin by greeting the applicant and talking to develop rapport. Explain what will be occurring and how long it will take. Explain that you want to ask about the applicant's interests, background, skills, career objectives, and past job performance. Let the candidate know you will allow enough time for questions at the end. Tell the applicant there will not be a decision at the end of the interview. This information sharing takes the pressure off both the candidate and the interviewer.

Briefly describe the position, but do not tell too much. Simply describing the position, who it reports to, and a brief account of duties should be sufficient. Be careful not to tell too much or tell precisely what you are looking for in a candidate. Using superlatives such as "aggressive" and "results driven" to describe the company, or statements such as, "You will aggressively call for new business," can communicate to the candidate what you are looking for. By keeping the position and the company's desires for filling the position vague, you may entice the candidate to reveal more about himself or herself.

As a courtesy, it is a good idea to ask for permission to take notes. This request will also convey that what the candidate says is important and will remove the candidate's fear that he or she said something wrong when you write information down.

Body of the Interview

You could begin with a statement such as, "Tell me about yourself." Responses to open-ended questions can be very revealing. Before a lot of information has been disclosed about the company and the position, responses to open-ended questions tend to indicate the candidate's true feelings or bias.

During the interview, focus questions on past job performance, background, and career objectives. Probe the *musts* to be sure the background listed on the application is solid.

Be sure to verify key skills and knowledge required for the position. Look for specific examples of the competencies required by the position. Have a consistent list of questions for every person. This will easily allow one candidate to be compared to others.

Realize that *musts* and *preferreds* are different. Don't become enamored with a glamorous *preferred*. Experience with a particular competitor may overshadow *musts* and make the candidate appear better than she or he is.

Be sure to bring your questions to a conclusion in time to allow the candidate to ask questions. Note the type and tone of questions the candidate asks. The type and tone may be more telling than the questions themselves. Also, examine these questions in light of the candidate's preparation, concerns, and motivation.

Summary and Close

It is important in closing an interview to thank the applicant for his or her time and interest. Recognize the effort required to take time off, prepare, dress, and come to the job interview. Compliment several strong points of the candidate. Inform the individual that several others will be interviewed, and give the candidate a sense of when and how he or she will hear the results of the interview.

After the applicant departs, complete your interview evaluation immediately. Do this while the interview is the freshest in your mind. History shows the last person interviewed gets the greatest consideration because the manager remembers the most about him or her.

It is important after the interview to keep commitments. Be sure to notify everyone, in writing, of the status of his or her candidacy. Lack of follow-up after an interview can ruin a good impression and tarnish the reputation of the organization. Remember, many of those interviewed may later become customers or be in positions to affect the company.

Conducting the Interview

First impressions are very powerful, but don't let them unduly influence you and cause you to make your decision too early.

It's important to keep an open mind during the interview and not to jump to conclusions too early. In the first few seconds after meeting another person, people form an opinion. From that point on, it takes more to change the opinion than it does to reinforce the impression. Try to reserve judgment throughout the interview and give full consideration to all that occurs. The appropriate time to make the decision about hiring someone is after the interview has taken place and objective comparisons can be made.

Focus on past job performance with specific questions to determine actual duties and responsibilities, conditions of performance, and level of performance. Note that meeting a set of objectives under very adverse conditions is a higher-level performance criterion than meeting the same objectives or goals under very positive conditions. Don't waste your time or the candidate's time with irrelevant questions. Stay focused on the performance and the attributes that were used to accomplish the performance.

Probe to be sure the individual's past performance has adequate examples of the attributes needed to perform in the position. Look for examples of what motivated or demotivated the candidate's performance. Probe for any criteria that could limit performance or cause harm, such as previous felony convictions or a poor driving record. Ensure all red flags or concerns have been addressed. The time to uncover future problems is before the hiring decision is made.

Evaluation of Candidate

As soon as the interview evaluation is completed, it is time to make a decision on whether to recommend that the individual be hired. Begin the evaluation by confirming examples of performance in previous positions. Remember, if the person just interviewed does not satisfactorily meet all criteria then he or she is no longer a candidate. Rate the candidate in terms of attributes, background, and other factors for the position. When completing the evaluation, you should also identify areas or issues to be probed or verified during reference and background checks. Immediately writing down the questions or points to check later prevents important information from being overlooked.

Off-Limits Areas

Certain types of questions must be off limits. It is not actually illegal to ask any question, but it is illegal to use prohibited information in making a decision. However, if something is asked, it can be argued that the information was a factor or at least influenced the decision. Based on this premise, do not ask any questions about the following:

- Race, color, gender, religion, age, national origin, or citizenship information
- Age-related questions such as birth date or date of high school graduation (unless verifying valid age requirement)
- Future family plans, career path of spouse, or activities of children
- Membership in clubs
- Height, weight, or physical description
- Previous foreign addresses
- Previous Workman's Compensation claims
- Past or present physical condition not related to essential job functions
- Arrest record or criminal convictions (if not felony or related to the position)

Many interviewers feel if the applicant volunteers information it is "fair game" and they may explore it further. If off-limits information is offered, it is best to not acknowledge the comment, continue the interview, steer the individual back to a job-related topic, and continue the interview. Be aware that an applicant might volunteer information and then, if rejected, file a charge of discrimination. Even a simple comment like, "Oh that's interesting," might cause a disgruntled applicant to claim the subject was discussed in the interview. The best response would be, "That is not considered in making a hiring decision. Let's move on to an area that is considered."

Interview Red Flags

Occasionally statements will be made which may indicate the presence of a situation that needs to be clarified before the individual is hired. These red flags are statements or reactions that occur during interviews. Some examples are

- The company had management problems
- They favored others in promotion . . . territory assignment. . . .
- I am not progressing as fast as others/as I should
- Not enough opportunity at the company . . . for promotion
- Any cash or merchandise handling problems
- Any situations that could result from ethics problems
- Lack of a sound reason for termination
- Job was just temporary
- I don't really remember
- Vague description of duties and responsibilities
- Lack of concrete details on how they performed

A red flag does not mean that a person is not a good candidate or would not perform well; it is a trigger for the interviewer and raises a degree of concern. These and any other red flags should be probed and clarified during interviews or in later reference checks. If these questions are not resolved by the time the person is hired, the cause of the red flag may become painfully obvious. By then, it is usually too late, and there will have been significant cost to the company. Many employers have regretted hiring someone without resolving a red flag. Later they realized the red flag was the proverbial tip of the iceberg and was a real indication of a severe problem.

Interview Strategies

There are a number of strategies an interviewer can employ to improve the quality of the interview and increase its effectiveness. Examples of strategies that increase effectiveness include:

Avoid talking too much. Limit the conversation to job-related topics. A good rule of thumb is that the candidate should talk 80 percent of the time or more, which means the interviewer must be silent all but 10–20 percent of the time.

Provide short, non-committal responses. One of the biggest time wasters is providing elaborate responses or commenting on the candidate's answers. The more the interviewer talks, the more he or she will telegraph the response to the answer. A poker face can be good at a game table but a warm, non-committal response is great in an interview. These techniques prevent the candidate from learning from your responses and possibly determining the "right" way to answer the next question.

Limit interruptions. Block out time and hold all phone calls. If the interview must be conducted in a public place such as a restaurant or a busy workplace, position yourself with your back to the area of greatest distraction. This positioning will give you the advantage of being able to focus more on the candidate.

Take notes while the candidate is talking. This technique is an excellent way not only to record responses but also to plan follow-up questions for later during the interview or reference checks.

Ask for other people's observations and/or impressions. Many candidates put their best foot forward during the actual interview but let their guard down with others such as the receptionist or personnel coordinator. At one large company the personnel assistant, who administered the pre-employment evaluations, many times saw an entirely different side of the candidate. Find out how a candidate treats others.

Listen carefully to responses. Many interviewers begin preparing their next question before the candidate has completed the response to the current question. The last several words of a candidate's response can dramatically change its meaning. Pause after the candidate's response to ensure he or she has finished. This pause also gives you time to react and develop the next question.

Suggested Actions for Improving the Interview Process

1. Examine those who have been hired in the last year to see how well their past job performance was uncovered. Compare what was learned in the interviews to their actual performance since being hired.
2. Examine the questions used in screening interviews to see if they uncover all the information needed. If not, create new screening interview questions.
3. Observe an in-depth interview by someone else. List strengths and weaknesses and how the interview could be improved.
4. Reconsider who has the buy-off authority to endorse or approve a hiring decision. Should this authority be revised, and if so, how?
5. Review the employment files of the last ten people hired and evaluate interview worksheets to see if they were completed at the conclusion of the interview. Were they detailed and accurate?

6. Develop the list of questions for each key position to assist in preparation.
7. Examine how screening interviews are conducted and determine improvements the next time they are conducted.
8. Examine the location where interviews are conducted to make sure it is quiet, free from distractions, private, and comfortable. Find a better location if needed.
9. Determine if interviewers have been telling the applicant too much, too soon in the interview.
10. Ensure that the observations from the interviews are written after the interview.
11. Mentally review recent interviews and see if you asked questions that were prohibited. If so, what were they?
12. Review the last several interviews and identify any interview red flags not resolved.
13. Next time an interview is conducted, ensure that the applicant talks 80 percent of the time.

Summary

The purpose of an interview is to understand the candidate's previous job duties and responsibilities, under what conditions the individual performed, and what the real level of performance was compared to standards and peers. Look for examples of the job attributes displayed in past positions. By examining an applicant's career goals and past job performance, the interviewer is able to make an informed judgment of the individual's potential for success in the position. Past performance is the best indicator of future performance. Performance is *the* criteria for selection. Developing and improving interview skills is an excellent use of a manager's time. The quality of the interview determines the manager's ability to make an effective selection.

We turn now to Billy Mullins, president of the Vikus Corporation, for an in-depth look at computer-aided job analysis and computer-assisted selection processes. Mullins is an expert in building software to assist employers in the hiring process as well as in analyzing the data various computer-aided analysis systems provide. Mullins correctly points out that even the best analysis tools will be useless if used improperly or if the data they provide is understood imperfectly. In his chapter, Mullins simplifies what can sometimes seem a dauntingly complicated process.

8

Computer-Aided Job Analysis and Selection

Billy Mullins II, M.S.

A New Approach to an Old Problem

What gets measured gets done. With that in mind, we developed systems that improve and streamline human resource decisions, liberating managers from the burden of repetitive tasks. Our systems are based on practical operations and personnel management expertise combined with modern information technology.

In today's competitive economy, organizations must gather and interpret more information than ever before. We bring focus to this task by helping managers gather and apply relevant information needed to make quicker, higher-quality human resource (HR) decisions. One of the most important places to start this data gathering is with the process of position analysis.

Job Analysis—The Link Between HR Management and Organizational Objectives

Position analysis is the foundation of human resource management. By clearly understanding a job and its requirements, an employer can more effectively select employees, evaluate job performance, target training, redesign work, and develop compensation plans. Position analysis is the glue that connects human resource management with the employer's business objectives, strategies, and the bottom line.

Without a systemic way to gather and organization information, job analysis is labor-intensive and time consuming. The position analysis process is a unique, computer-assisted

• Position Content	• the activities of the position (duties and tasks)
• Position Requirements	• knowledge, skills, and abilities (KSA)
	• years of experience
	• education, degrees, and licenses
• Position Content	• purpose of the job
	• degree of accountability or responsibility
	• extent of supervision received and/or exercised
	• consequences of error
	• physical demands and working conditions

method that arms you with the critical job information you need to effectively manage your workforce. Position analysis is the process of gathering, documenting, and analyzing information about three basic aspects of a job.

Valid and valuable position analysis information can usually be gathered in a day of structured interviews with a supervisor and three top performers in the job. Once the process is complete, it is quick, easy, and inexpensive to update.

Position analysis will enable you to take an integrated approach to human resource management and help you align your efforts with the critical, strategic issues of your business. Unlike many *job* analysis processes that are designed for managing a single human resource function, our position analysis process can provide critical information for eight major HR functions.

• Position Design	• Performance Appraisals
• Compensation	• Performance Maintenance
• Structured Selection	• Employment Development
• Skills Training	• Safety and Ergonomics

We gather the position data at the *duty* level. This approach allows us to tie eight important aspects to each duty.

• Task Statements	• Skills
• Physical Demands and Hazards	• Ability
• Education and Experience	• Compensation
• Knowledge	• Beliefs and Convictions

Powered with this level of information, we are then able to:

- Design and redesign positions as needed
- Value (price) each duty and ultimately the position within the structure of the organization
- Identify required and desired levels of knowledge and skills for each duty
- Select candidates who meet those required skill levels
- Identify and measure critical performance for each duty
- Identify critical safety training required for each duty

Employee Selection— New Rules of the Game

Have you ever enjoyed playing or watching a game without understanding the rules? Have you ever been confused or simply left in the dark about your own job responsibilities? Does it surprise you that the employees in today's workforce will quit your job and have another before the day is over, if they do not "like" what they are doing?

Not very long ago, an employers' market existed—there were more applicants than job openings. The purpose of a selection process was to simply predict the best performing applicant from a pool of the most qualified people. Little effort was made to predict how well the applicant would "fit" with both the job and the culture. If the new employee did not fit, there were plenty of waiting replacements.

Today, we find ourselves in an employees' market. The employees have all the options. Unemployment rates are near an all-time low. Baby boomers are beginning to retire, and the workforce is shrinking. Members of the emerging workforce seem less willing to stay in a job that they dislike. Job satisfaction is often more important to them than pay. They are more loyal to their skill set than to their employer. Consequently, organizations are facing turnover like they have never experienced before. Without a stable workforce, employers find performance goals very difficult to achieve. The enormous but heretofore often overlooked cost of non-fit turnover is finally getting the attention of top management.

Although the employment landscape has changed dramatically, many organizations have not. In fact, many human resource practitioners and academicians continue to believe that the sole purpose of a selection system is to predict the performance of job applicants.

In today's economic and labor environment, it is imperative for professionals managing an employment selection process to predict not just performance, but also tenure. Predicting performance deals with the issues of "can do"—the knowledge, skills, and technical abilities required for the job. Where improvement is needed is in the assessment of the fit of a candidate with the job and the employer's culture. In other words, they will be able to predict tenure by assessing the issues of "will do."

So how does an organization go about predicting both performance and tenure? We suggest using modern scientific methods and tools that have heretofore been underutilized in human resource management.

A Systems View

Viewed from a process perspective, all organizations are made up of a number of interdependent systems. Many leaders fail to step back and realize that there are some basic principles that govern all systems.

1. Since systems are interconnected, you can never "fix" a system with one solution.
2. Structure produces behavior.
3. Causes are usually separated in time and space from results.
4. Every system is perfectly designed for the results it is getting.

Both empirical and descriptive evidence suggests that many

employee selection systems fail to meet their most basic objective—matching applicants (each with their own unique skills, interests, and attitudes) to the skills and abilities required by the job.

Companies involved in selecting employees (both internally and externally) must gather, store, and interpret more information than ever before. However, it is not just a matter of moving more data faster. The key is to create value by using information to make better decisions.

It is clear that many current organizational practices, which worked so well in the more predictable and lower-tech economy of the 1950's to 1980's, have little utility in today's faster paced, information driven economy. The magnitude of these changes means that many organizations are being forced to change their processes, and even transform their cultures, just to be competitive in today's markets. The time has come to use technology to gather and organize information so that even non-experts can apply it to achieve expert quality results.

Time for a Change

Interviewing job applicants is one process that is particularly vulnerable to the subjective biases, prejudices, and stereotypes of the human interviewer. The result of this subjectivity is that the organization often misses the opportunity to employ the most qualified candidate.

In 1984, Drs. Hunter and Hunter published an article in *Psychological Bulletin* titled "Validity and Utility of Alternative Predictors of Job Performance."[1] Based on extensive research about the predictive value of various selection tools, these researchers reported the following correlation coefficients between various selection tools and an employee's ultimate performance on the job.

- Random Selection 09
- Interview 11

- Structured Interview 21
- Job Try-Out 44

The wealth of knowledge contained in this little table warrants further explanation. If you hired every third person that walked in your door, this random selection would predict about 9 percent of the new hire's performance. If you conducted a traditional, non-structured interview, you would predict about 11 percent of performance—not much better than random selection. If, however, you structure the interview (ask all the applicants the same questions so you can directly compare them), you would predict 21 percent of performance—nearly double the value of a non-structured interview. Finally, if you gave applicants a *content valid* job tryout (that is, one that represents the critical functions of the job), your process would predict about 44 percent of performance.

Improving Decisions by Structuring the Employee Selection Process

Today, the ultimate structured interview is a computer-aided interview. Research indicates that job applicants are more honest in answering questions asked by computers than they are with human interviewers. A computer can gather 15 times more information than a human interviewer can in the same amount of time and can organize this information in meaningful reports that are available immediately. Armed with this information, the face-to-face interviewer can focus in on specific areas of concern and significantly increase the predictive value of the interview.

By viewing organizations as systems and considering the empirical evidence of the value of structuring an interview, it is logical to conclude that structuring the entire selection process can significantly improve the value of the process. Taking this logic a step further, the process should be structured like a funnel—start with the lowest cost screening tools at the top of the funnel and progress through the tools until the final screen is given to the most viable candidates.

The following is one recommended sequence of screening processes that has been used successfully by a number of organizations.

Pre-job Offer

- Take applications
- Conduct a computer-aided interview
- Conduct a follow-up face-to-face interview
- Conduct a reference/background check
- Conduct a job tryout (Realistic Position Demonstration [RPD])

Post-job Offer

Supervisory performance review three times during the probationary period, usually the first 12 weeks of employment

Using Technology to Gather and Process Applicant Data

Our Structured Selection Process™ (SSP) is the computer-automated version of the screening process described above. This process includes our proven applicant screening method along with definitions of objective measures, including criteria measures through the probationary period.

Applying our expertise in industrial/organizational psychology, our firm has developed proprietary software that enables a computerized and customized interview system. This system provides extensive, immediate feedback in a concise report that makes human interviews more productive and facilitates quick decisions. The feedback includes targeted and legally defensible follow-up questions based on an applicant's responses.

This computer-aided interview (CAI) is not a test. It is a highly structured interview that equips managers with information needed to make the best hiring decisions. The CAI uses 16 scales to predict performance and tenure.

• Attendance	• Biographical
• Counterproductive Behavior	• Education
• Employment History	• Flexibility
• Honesty	• Locus of Control
• Manageability	• Negative Affectivity
• Proactive Personality	• Quantity/Quality
• Safety	• Teamwork
• Work Ethic	• Job Specific

Another key component of the Structured Selection Process is a Realistic Position Demonstration. An RPD is an exercise developed to require an applicant to demonstrate his or her ability to perform one or more of a job's critical functions.

The SSP software enables you to analyze qualified candidates, as compared to a profile of existing employees in that job classification. Ninety percent of Baldridge Award winning companies profile their current employees and use that information to analyze applicants for job openings. We apply the profiling concept to both the CAI and the RPD, giving your company an objective tool to compare the unknown (the applicant) to the known (current employees who meet your expectations).

The Structured Selection Process revolutionizes employee selection. It provides an extensive measurement toolkit. Armed with the progressive information of the SSP, you have readily available the information you need to measure and report utilization for both EEO1[2] and OFCCP[3] flow statistics. Furthermore, we provide seven critical measures enabling you to communicate more effectively to your organization in bottom line business terms.

- Selectivity—ratio of interviews to hires
- Quality of Applicant (CAI)—ratio of applicants that meet the job profile
- Quality of Applicant (RPD)—ratio of applicants that meet the job profile
- Quality of Hire—ratio of new hires that meet or exceed performance expectations
- Nonfit Turnover Rate—bad hires
- New Hire Turnover Rate—all probationary turnover
- Total Turnover (all company turnover)—probationary and non-probationary)

Summary

Historically, most of the time and money spent on the employee selection process has been reactive—dealing with both legal and operational problems caused by bad hiring decisions. Experience has proven, however, that paying attention to selection on the front-end can not only save much of the time and money spent dealing with problems, but can also help managers stay focused on their primary objective of providing quality goods and services to customers.

Remember system principle number four, "Every system is perfectly designed for the results it is getting." Albert Einstein once said, "The definition of insanity is doing the same thing over and over and expecting different results." Is it time for you to review your current selection process?

Notes

1. "Validity and Utility of Alternative Predictors of Job Performance," John E. Hunter and Rhonda F. Hunter, *Psychological Bulletin* 96(1), 72–98.

2. EEO1 is the Equal Employment Opportunity Form 1 document required by the government reporting the company's applicant flow.
3. OFCCP stands for the Office of Federal Contracts and Compliance Policy. If a company has federal contracts, OFCCP requires a set of flow statistics.

With Wayne Outlaw's hiring theories and Billy Mullins' computer-aided staffing ideas in mind, we turn now to Joyce Gioia for a look at how best to implement the orientation process once you've extended an offer to an employee. Gioia, president of the Herman Group and co-editor of this volume, suggests that the period of orientation can be your most important opportunity to bond with your employees. This bond may well be the cornerstone of a long and fruitful relationship between workers and the company, and is key to achieving the retention so valuable in today's shifting marketplace. She covers all aspects of the orientation process from facilities tours to ways that make the process more enjoyable for all.

9

Orientation and Bonding

Joyce Gioia, M.B.A., CMC

Orientation: Your Opportunity to Bond with New Hires

We used to take orientation for granted. It was a necessary evil, an annoyance that we tolerated in order to get people "on board." We knew we needed to give them information about our benefits programs, our company policies, and where the rest rooms were. We introduced the new employees to their co-workers, their supervisors, and other departments with which they interacted. Beyond that, new employees were left to learn the culture and fend for themselves. If new employees didn't stay, it was "No problem." There were lots more good people waiting to come to work for us.

Life is different now. There aren't lots of good people waiting to work for us anymore. The worker shortages that plague corporate America have caused the labor market to do a 180-degree turn. It's a sellers' market for labor now. People can pick and choose the companies they want to work for. Now, if you don't give them an adequate orientation, if they don't feel valued, they'll simply leave. New hire turnover is at an all time high.

It has become *vital* to use the orientation time to begin "bonding" with new hires, to begin developing their close relationship to your company. You want to lay a foundation to build up their loyalty to the company. (For more information about the bonding process, see chapter 14, "Internal Marketing.")

The Emerging Corporate Culture

With the labor shortages giving employees more choices, corporate cultures are evolving to be more employee-centered. Organizations are becoming aware that they can no longer operate in the ways they did in the past. They will find themselves unable to recruit the workers they'll need to get the job done. Not surprisingly, orientation has had to change with the times.

A new model based on our changing times was needed, a model that makes new employees feel important and helps them understand the value they bring to the organization. In addition, this new orientation must give them *all* they need to know about your employee benefit program and inculcate them with your culture.

Our Model for the Ideal Orientation

Our model for the ideal orientation is just that, an ideal. You may discover that some element of our model is not necessary or appropriate to your circumstances. Please do not feel that it is imperative to include everything that we suggest. We suggest these elements only because they have worked for other companies in the past.

The Introduction and "Reinforce the Sale"

Do you welcome new hires to your organization as if they were honored guests? Do you make them feel like you're happy to see them? Recognize that new employees arrive on the first day feeling excited and a little fearful. Orientation can alleviate those fears or make them worse. Is there one individual assigned to each of the new hires to help them feel more comfortable and to help them get acclimated?

One of the fears that new hires have is "Did I make the *right* decision?" They wonder, "Did I take the right job offer for me?" Orientation is also your opportunity to "reinforce the sale." It's your chance to reassure new workers that they made the right decision by accepting your job offer over the others.

Plant/Office Tour

Next, we recommend a tour of the facility. Whether the new hire is beginning work in an office or a plant, a complete tour will allow you to introduce the individual to someone in each of the departments. While there, let the department representative tell the new employee about the department, its functions, how it interacts with other departments (especially the new hire's department), and the part it plays in affecting the bottom line of the organization. Some organizations then have that department representative escort the new hire to the next department. Wherever possible, a logical sequencing of departments will help the neophyte better understand the big picture and how his or her job fits into that picture.

One company we know provides new hires with a "passport" that they must get stamped or initialed by each of the executives they are scheduled to visit. When their passports are full, they redeem them for a small gift with the company logo. Using a passport ensures that each new hire will have an opportunity to personally relate with a handful of the executives. This process goes a long way toward making the individual feel important and valued.

Communicate the Significance
of the Individual's Contribution

Most employees, whether they have worked for a company for a long time or a short one, do not really understand the way corporations work. They have no concept of what it costs to hire and train, to buy raw materials, to sell the products. Most also have no sense for the importance of their contributions to the bottom line.

This orientation time can be your chance to communicate that importance, before the people even report to their specific job sites. (For more information about how to communicate that significance, see chapter 13, "Inspiring Front-line Workers."

Training Within Orientation

Your organization believes in continuous learning, right? What better way to drive that point home than by including some sort of training in your orientation? We're not talking about skills training here. That's important, too, but later. For the time being, we're talking about some sort of short course—an hour or two is enough—in some area that is work-related, but not directly job-related.

Some examples of courses we're talking about are handling difficult people, time management, or behavioral styles training. We're suggesting some learning that will help the individual feel like the time was *personally* well spent, that is, no matter what the individual does in later life, the information learned will be valuable. This personal enhancement training is especially important if you hold your orientation on a Saturday, considered by most to be "personal time."

Present People Who Have *Been There*

Do you have mid- or executive-level individuals on your staff who started out in the same ground floor positions that your new hires are taking? Demonstrating this kind of career "pathing" will help reinforce their good decisions to choose your employment. When college seniors were asked what was the most important criteria to them in choosing a new employer, number one was the ability to grow. If your new hires see and hear for themselves that others who started where they are starting have risen through the ranks, that will go a long way toward confirming that they made the right decisions.

Also, these folks who have "been there" and "done that" will be ingeniously communicating your culture. This presentation time may be your new hires' first chance to meet others from your organization, to see how employees respect and relate with each other.

Assigning Buddies, Sponsors, and Mentors

Another excellent idea is to pair up your new hires with buddies, sponsors, or mentors. When you assign new workers a peer or a more senior employee to work with, you can significantly shorten the time it takes for an individual to become productive. When new hires immediately have someone they can comfortably ask questions, they feel more relaxed—and will therefore become more easily acclimated.

Assigning mentors sends a clear signal that you want to help people grow, that you are ready to invest in them, and that you want to see them succeed. There's also something about the dynamic between mentor and mentee that encourages growth—for both parties. The mentee grows because he or she wants to please the mentor, and the mentor grows because it's important to continuously provide the right role model. Mentor-mentee programs are definitely win-win-win. The mentees and mentors grow, and the company enjoys the advantage of having more capable employees.

Include an Appearance by One of the Executives

When an executive appears at an orientation, particularly when that person conveys the welcome message, workers feel valued. The company thinks enough of them to have one of the executives participate in their orientation. This appearance, too, reinforces the sale.

Here are some suggested topics the executive might talk about.

- Their pleasure at seeing the new hires (welcome)
- The myriad of growth opportunities the organization offers
- The mission, vision, and values of the organization
- The corporate culture

Gift Them with Some Tangible Item

It's a good idea to end your group orientation by giving each employee a small gift—a coffee mug or mouse pad for their desks, a T-shirt or gym bag, or some other tangible gift that says you are happy to have them on board. The gift does not have to be costly; it's the thought that counts.

This investment in your new hires also gives them a tangible reflection of your esteem. Imagine the scene when your new employee comes home to the family with a gift from the first day of work! While it's not uncommon for employees to earn gifts and recognition after they have been with the company for a while, it is unusual for them to receive a gift in the first few days. Your thoughtful token is a nice gesture. You want your new hire to be excited, happy, and raring to go!

The Longer the Orientation, the Stronger the Bond

We were able to significantly reduce new hire turnover when we supported a client to change their orientation from two hours to six. Of course, just changing the length of time was far from the whole story. They also implemented much of the orientation model we have just discussed, but we believe that the length of time played a major role.

Why? Because the longer the orientation, the more time you have with new hires to positively reinforce their decision to work for your company, to help them feel connected to your organization, to help them feel valued, and to instill your culture.

Orientation to the Department or Job Function

Orientation should not end with the group time. New hire and supervisor need to spend some quality time together— before the employee is expected to begin being productive. A strong connection with the supervisor can speed the learning of both skills and culture and surely can reduce the time until the employee becomes productive.

Supervisors Should Review the Mission, Vision, and Values

Investing the time in the first hours of work to talk about the mission, vision, and values for the organization and/or the department can have a very positive effect on the learning curve. The supervisor should talk about the mission and how the new hire can express that mission through his or her work. Suggest that the new worker consider what contribution he or she can make to the vision of the organization.

As a society, we base our decisions on our values. Our values reflect what is important to us. Companies are human collaborations; they base their decision about corporate values on their individual values as well. Thus, it's important to discuss each of the values separately: why the company chose it, what it means, and how it is expressed in the day-to-day work.

Good Time to Clarify Expectations, Set Goals, and Offer a Growth Program

This quality time with new hires is the perfect time to clarify expectations, help the new worker set SMART goals, and work together on an agreed on "growth program." SMART goals are specific, measurable, achievable, realistic, and timed. Many psychologists will tell you that a misunderstanding regarding expectations is the most common reason for a breakdown in relationships. Clarifying expectations between supervisor and worker will go a long way toward strengthening that relationship. When people know what's expected of them, they are much more able to follow through and provide those actions, activities, or levels of performance. Not having to guess also makes employees feel more secure and more likely to stay.

One of our clients likes to draw a "T" on a single blank page. On the left is what the new hire can reasonably expect from the company; on the right is what the company expects from him or her. On the right side of the page are expectations such as "being responsible to follow through with commitments," "getting to work on time," and "letting some person of authority know if something is wrong." On the left side of the page are incentives such as "as much software training as you want," "business cards after six months," "bonus after one year," and "referral fees when your friends are hired."

The supervisor needs to work with the new hires to help them develop short- and long-term SMART goals. If the goals aren't SMART, new hires may be set up for failure, or at least the parties may not be aware of achievement.

If your organization offers career "pathing," and even if it doesn't, the supervisor needs to work with the individual to develop what we call "a personal growth program." Tailored to the individual, this program gives the new hire a blueprint for his or her work with the company over the next three months, six months, or one year. The program provides a road map for the person's growth, including skills and courses that the individual wants to acquire and timelines for acquiring those skills and abilities.

Orientation Should Be Fun!

Yes, of course your orientation must be a time of learning, but it can also be fun. You can include crossword puzzles, games, and other devices to get your new hires involved with the information they *must* learn during your orientation. You can strengthen the learning about topics such as your sexual harassment policy and benefits by including these kinds of games.

One of our clients even includes a behind-the-scenes tour of Madison Square Garden. They hold the orientation right across the street in their offices. New hires love getting to see the locker rooms first hand. The tour makes new employees feel very special.

Though this model for orientation may seem involved and extensive, we know that it is very cost effective. With recruiting costs at an all time high and the cost of turnover being what it is, your investment in an extensive orientation will more than pay for itself!

Sylvia Gaffney has 15 years of experience in the staffing and outplacement industries, and is an expert in organizational development. Her areas of specialty include organizational effectiveness and change management. In the next chapter, Gaffney addresses the use of career development as a retention tool, moving from Joyce Gioia's ideas about orientation bonding to her own theories regarding how to retain your newly hired employees. Gaffney writes that fully assessing and discussing career plans and opportunities with your employees creates a stronger and more productive internal workforce. She gives you still more ways to grow, groom, and keep your people.

10

Career Development as a Retention and Succession Planning Tool

Sylvia Gaffney, M.S.O.D.

Overview

Internal career development programs are proving critical in keeping valued employees while concurrently ensuring greater control over the succession planning process. Retention research indicates that individuals tend to stay longer where they experience personal and professional growth. Internal career development is instrumental in providing that vehicle for growth. Employers who actively partner with their employees in aligning career direction with company goals realize better retention rates. Also, employees involved in a career plan for their personal development report more satisfaction with their work and tend to stay longer.

The synergy between career development and succession planning creates an ongoing business strategy that incorporates retention and succession planning as part of the systemic organizational structure. Internal career development, training initiatives, mentoring, coaching, evaluations, annual reviews, and orientation programs are meaningfully connected to organizational goals. The result is a workable process that consistently addresses the corporate requirements for finding, keeping, and placing talent in key positions as needed. The organization experiences positive bottom-line results while preparing for future business needs based on mutual corporate and individual growth.

Case for Career Development and Succession Planning Synergies

Viewing career development in conjunction with succession planning provides the organization and the individual with what is needed and wanted by both employer and employee. Each side of the equation perceives a reciprocal win.

The traditional career paths of yesterday defined a point-to-point progression that targeted a select few for specific leadership positions. Career management pathing-programs generally worked because the environment was more static, jobs were more stable, and employees were more loyal and connected to their organization. These conditions do not describe today's workplace. Job jumping, career changing, volatile industries, and shifting work environments are now a way of organizational life. The implicit contracts between employer and employee have significantly changed. What can be done to overcome these challenges?

When employees understand what the organization needs and how their personal career aspirations fit into the overall plan, a new contract develops. When companies share the corporate vision with their employees beyond plaques on the wall, internal business partners are generated who have a vested interest in the success of the organization. The two-way information flow allows employer and employee awareness of what is wanted and needed from each other. Mutual expectations are clear. Companies know where they need strong players, and employees are realistically aware of *how* they fit into the corporations' bench strength requirements. The corporate dialogue is healthy, ongoing, and productive. The company can assess whether or not an individual is considered a possible player, and the employee can decide if he or she wants to be part of the game.

The tight job market requires creative solutions to succession challenges. These challenges have long existed in companies of all sizes, but in the modern marketplace, succession issues are now evolving into gigantic problems. Succession planning is becoming a major casualty in the retention drama. Organizations need to plan even more than ever before for their future brainpower needs.

Begin with Role Criticality Processing

One means of implementing this type of strategy is for the organization to define its succession planning process more broadly to include *all* the critical roles existing now, needed soon, and necessary in the future.

Each role in every department throughout the organization should be analyzed for its purpose and importance in the company. Each individual should be appraised for his or her unique retention risk. A company must know if the risk is high or low for losing someone who is crucial to the organization. Once critical roles and the availability of critical people can be assessed, a corporate-wide plan of action may be developed. The role criticality process requires you to ask these questions:

- What positions are needed now, and as we plan for the future?
- What do we need to do to retain and develop employees for current and projected needs?
- What is our plan for redundant and/or unnecessary roles?
- What is our approach for individuals who aren't doing well, but can be trained to improve?
- What will we do with individuals who are in critical roles, are at a low risk of leaving, but need to leave the organization for performance reasons?

Obviously, the support and involvement of top management is required. Human resources (HR) or any other single department cannot be "solo champions." A comprehensive process needs the support and endorsement of the executive team to lead the organization. The concept is a simple one. It involves a commitment to corporate and individual growth by employer and employee.

Utilize the Corporate Business Plan

An obvious place to begin is with a plan that is already in place; build from there. It's a workable methodology that utilizes the corporate business plan. It parallels the company goals and objectives with an employee's individual career plan.

Traditionally, the corporate business plan is carefully crafted and rarely discussed with anyone beyond management. This lack of discussion is understandable, since the plan's numbers are often used for forecasting financing initiatives. Top-level management and department heads usually have substantial input into them. Given that considerable time, thought, and planning energy has gone into the creation of these plans, it makes sense to expand their use to address the ever-growing need for talent in an organization.

When appropriate segments of the corporate business plan

are shared with employees, these individuals more completely understand their role in the successful implementation of the plan. It doesn't guarantee that employees realize everything they want when they want it. That expectation would be unrealistic, and that is simply not the way things work. The idea is to use the corporate business plan as the guiding instrument and encourage employees to understand themselves enough to know where and when they fit in.

The reality is that many of today's employees operate under the assumption that the company cares primarily about the bottom line. There has certainly been enough evidence of non-caring corporate behavior with all the downsizing, right-sizing, and restructuring experienced since the mid-1980's. Employees tend to see themselves more as corporate free agents, and act accordingly. They want and will have control over their careers. Rather than react negatively to employees' take-charge attitude, management should capitalize on it. Organizational leaders can leverage the investment they make in business plan creation through the synergy of connecting it to succession planning and internal career development. Here's how it works.

Craft an Individual Career Plan to Parallel the Company Plan

Introduce employees to the corporate business plan. They will learn that the company business plan is a selling document. It guides an organization through a reality check, from definition of its product to the direction it wants to go in the future. The plan clarifies what a company has to offer the marketplace. It outlines how the company will package, price, promote, and distribute its product or services. It describes the talent needed to deliver its product or service.

The employee can then assess what he or she wants to do in relation to what talent is currently required and will be required in the future of the organization. Individual responsibility is encouraged.

Companies benefit when they encourage employees to become entrepreneurial about their careers. These employees assume the primary responsibility for growth and development of their own careers. They understand what it means to be "high-ticket items" that need to provide a valued service within their company. Employees understand that while they are primarily responsible for their own careers, partnering with the company in attaining its goals is highly beneficial. The process of paralleling the corporate business plan with the individual career plan requires the commitment of initial set-up time.

For employees to become genuinely invested in an organization's plan, they need to understand not only what the company wants to accomplish, but also need to be specific about what they currently have to offer. It's also essential that the individuals plan for what *they* want to achieve in the future. This point is where the parallel process of internal career development comes into play.

Begin with Corporate and Self-Assessment

An internal career development program begins with assessment. The organization needs to understand what it is all about. The employees within the organization need to understand what they are all about. The component parts need to know how they all fit together.

Organizational assessment necessarily starts at the top with senior management and other key stakeholders. It goes beyond thoughtful understanding and clear articulation of the corporate plan. It involves designing a systemic process in which all things support and fit with each other. The components necessary for organizational understanding are complete knowledge of: purpose, direction, financial objectives, strategy, structure, management, external issues, internal issues, and its culture.

- PURPOSE: What is the company mission, its reason for being in existence?

- DIRECTION: What are the short- and long-term objectives that provide a stable direction for the organization, allowing it to realize its purpose?
- FINANCIAL OBJECTIVES: What are the metrics that need to be studied, projected, and met for the organization to realize its long-term sustainability?
- STRATEGY: What are the plans and resources that differentiate the organization and give it its competitive edge in the marketplace?
- STRUCTURE: What are all the systems, processes, policies, and procedures within the organization that support the business strategy?
- MANAGEMENT: What are the capabilities, style, and approach its leaders have to communication, decision making, and interaction with other members of the organization?
- EXTERNAL ISSUES: What is going on in the environment that creates opportunities or threats that could positively or negatively affect the strategy?
- INTERNAL ISSUES: What strengths, weaknesses, core competencies, and resources exist or are deficient within the organization?
- CULTURE: How are things done, and who and what really matters in this organization?

Once these concepts and objectives are completely understood, employees are then guided through a program in which they define *their* skills, values, strengths, interests, education, experiences, exposures, natural resources, developmental gaps, goals, and other pieces of the puzzle that make up the individual person.

- SKILLS: What skills have you developed and used in the past that you enjoy utilizing, and want to offer this organization in the future work you do here?
- VALUES: Where and how do you expend your time, energy, and money?

- STRENGTHS: What describes the unique essence of you that goes to the heart of your expertise and characterizes those abilities in which you are the most proficient?
- INTERESTS: What is and has been fun and provides an excitement dimension in your work life?
- EDUCATION: What are the formal and informal learning opportunities that have molded your thinking process to be what it is today?
- EXPERIENCES: What are the bitter and sweet things that have occurred in your life that contribute to what it means to be you?
- EXPOSURES: Where have you been, and what unusual things have you seen and done?
- NATURAL RESOURCES: What works for or against you by virtue of the way you look, sound, or smell?
- DEVELOPMENTAL GAPS: What is lacking in your personal and professional growth?
- GOALS: What do you want out of life and wish to be remembered for by the people you care about?

Specifically, individual values and goals are examined and compared to the corporate culture and organizational goals. For the synergy to occur most effectively, management needs to be aware of the basic assumptions, values, norms, and artifacts that exist in the organization. The outcome of the assessment phase is corporate and self-awareness.

A Workable System That Grows, Grooms, and Keeps Employees

By paralleling self-assessment to the corporate business plan, employees gain clarity about the organizational culture, goals, strategy, and structure. It becomes clearer how and where they fit in, and they can then know if what they are doing is what they want to do. Employers stay on top of and in touch with the human resources that are currently available, and what each person offers, and they will also know when employees are ready for a mutually beneficial move within the organization.

Since individuals are aligning themselves to situations where they will grow and develop, it makes sense for the organization to be part of that development. It's an effective and efficient process once in place. Managers work with their direct reports on an on-going basis to manage mutual expectations and company realities.

The overworked cliché, the "win-win proposition," works well here. When these strategies are implemented, companies *grow, groom, and keep* the people they need, for what they need and when they need them. Employees are happier making responsible career choices. Mutual commitment is high. The initial investment requires management's dedication to align corporate structures and strategies to include an internal career development program. The stakes are high, but more than worth the effort. Since good employees remain longer in this type of environment, retention, and therefore succession planning, becomes a reality and an almost unquantifiable benefit.

Once you have employee career development goals firmly in place and aligned with your overall business goals, you can begin to explore specific ways of offering your employees training and education in order to enhance their value and your productivity. In the next chapter, Chad Cook focuses on organizational design and development strategies for workforce stability. He notes that as the workforce transforms from an employer dominated market to an employee controlled environment, the onus is on employers to provide incentives to stay with the company. In a market where knowledge is money, offering your employees opportunities to learn, train for, and utilize new skills can be crucial in your retention effort.

11

Training for Retention

Chad Cook, M.B.A.

Why Is Training and Development So Important for Employee Retention?

What do employees want? Why is there such a high turnover rate among skilled workers? In today's labor market, these are questions every business—yours included—must ask itself. Workers are the most important element of any business; they must be retained, and happily so, in order for the business to remain competitive. For your company to compete and to retain its workers, you must first understand what today's worker needs from his or her job.

Good Workers Want and Expect Career Growth

In reviewing many of the research studies to determine how to retain good workers, one consistent theme emerges:

employees want the opportunity for growth in their jobs. In surveys, employees articulate this desire in a variety of ways, but the desire is still the same. Some terms workers consistently use to describe their desires are

- Career promotion and growth opportunities
- Growth potential
- Training in the workplace
- Promotion and growth opportunities
- Coaching and feedback from the boss
- Opportunity to learn new skills
- Advancement opportunities

In fact, a 1999 Interim Consulting Study conducted by the Saratoga Institute found that "no perceived career growth opportunity" was the second most common reason for turnover. This study collected additional data from new college graduates to help clarify what attracts new workers to employers and found that "new graduates don't come to a company because it has career development—but they do not come if there is not career development." Put simply, employees want the opportunity for job and career growth in any employment situation. If this crucial desire is not fulfilled, they will leave.

The Emerging "I, Inc." Workforce

Economic Situation

The economy is good and there are many jobs available for good workers. As a consequence, good workers who don't feel valued by their current employers for anything more than "today's work output" pursue other job options. These workers possess knowledge, skills, and abilities that other employers are seeking. In fact, other employers will likely value them more by increasing their pay and providing them with new experiences—the opportunity to learn and grow.

By moving to a new employer, the worker becomes worth more in his or her own eyes and in the eyes of other employers. This rise in stature is, of course, quite appealing.

Allegiance

The employer/employee contract is weakening and good workers no longer feel an allegiance to an employer who is not investing in their personal growth. The well-worn axiom of "What have you done for me lately?" is being asked in reverse. Now, the good worker is asking this question of the employer. Good workers expect a challenging, safe job, with reasonable working conditions. They want input about how the job should be performed, and require the independence to perform the job in a professional yet individual manner. They also want comparable pay to others who hold similar positions, special recognition for excellent performance, continuous growth of skills and abilities, and some fun on the side. In the new workplace environment, the employer/employee relationship is certainly a two-way street.

On and Off the Job

Quality of work life is a higher priority to top performers than it has been in the recent past. Good workers expect to balance their work and personal life to meet their needs and the needs of the business. High performance expectations are challenging for good workers, but undue pressure to work long hours, to miss lunch, to travel endlessly, and to manage constantly changing priorities is no longer regarded as a "red badge of courage" that must be endured to be successful. It's too easy to locate another position where the work/life balance is more reasonable.

In fact, the option of becoming self-employed and contracting services back to the employer is becoming a popular alternative. This alternative is being facilitated by ever easier access to technology. Not all employees are looking to jump ship; this quest for independence is just an indication of how the new workforce is thinking. Helping employees balance the work/life mix is a developmental challenge that few organizations are confronting at present.

Need for Growth Opportunities

Good workers expect to grow to remain personally competitive in the job market. Employees' personal growth expectation impacts employers. Since the guarantee of job security has been eroded in the minds of employees, the concept of "lifetime employment" has changed to a concept of "lifetime employability." To support this new concept, good workers expect and seek out learning and improvement opportunities. However, these opportunities may not necessarily be formal training; they may also mean special assignments that stretch and improve skills, mentoring relationships, community assignments, college courses, certifications, professional memberships, and more.

How Can You Provide Career Growth and Training?

Strategic Choices

Match your training and development efforts to the strategic objectives of the company. Determine what goals your organization has, and what it will take to achieve them. You then have the alternative of (a) hiring the skills you need to accomplish these goals; or (b) developing the skills from within your current workforce. Link the strategic objectives for any training/development you create directly to the goals of the company, so that good workers understand how what they learn impacts the business. Clarifying the links between the desired outcomes and the developmental effort to be undertaken also will help the designer of the training/development effort to focus on the specific business outcomes to be achieved.

Being Goal-Oriented

Focus your training efforts on specific performance outcomes rather than on theory or "learning for the future." There are appropriate times and places for these other forms of development, but they are not appropriate when you're attempting to help a good worker improve performance or learn new performance behaviors.

Responsibility and Accountability

Assign the accountability for endorsing and supporting training/development to the participant's immediate supervisor. Often, much of the new knowledge and skills learned during training/development efforts is not applied on the job. The main reason for this failure is the result of adherence to and comfort with the "old routine." It's difficult to break old habits and apply the new knowledge and skills on the job.

The first opportunity to break this cycle is for the supervisor to meet with the participant prior to the development effort and jointly set expectations/goals for what will be learned, as well as for anticipated changes that will occur after the event. The second opportunity is for the supervisor to meet with the participant when the individual returns from the event, and jointly agree to specific application plans. Finally, the supervisor may monitor, follow, and coach the participant to bring the new applications to life.

Another option is for the participant to share his or her learning with others in the workgroup, so that they understand the changes being implemented, support the changes, and maybe even apply the changes themselves. Teaching what one has learned can often be very beneficial and helpful in the learning and training process.

Prepare for Success

Create a talent profiling process that supports succession planning and/or key talent bench strength processes within the organization. The talent profile provides assurances for good workers that their knowledge, skills, and experiences are documented and available for promotional decision making, special project assignments, and other tasks. The profile is also an indication that the organization values the employee's knowledge and skills for more than just the immediate job. Included on the talent profile can be the future aspirations of the employee, his or her education, previous work experiences, training/development, and performance appraisal ratings.

Continual Learning

Implement a company university program consisting of a series of core courses focused on the critical success factors for your organization. These courses may represent technical skills, relationship skills, basic supervision/management, leadership, team skills, basic business finance, continuous improvement skills, communication, conflict management, college courses, certifications, and associate degrees. Courses can be offered by both internal and external providers. They don't even have to be on-site. Just the fact that the company has defined, supports, and promotes a specified list of courses that align with the knowledge and skills required to be successful on the job, will assure employees that the organization wants them to learn, improve, and grow. Reimburse education and/or degrees that align with organizational needs.

In-house Mentors

Encourage mentoring relationships to help aspiring employees better understand what is required to advance and succeed within the company. Teach your supervisors/managers how to coach and support employees so they can achieve high performance standards and feel good about themselves, as well as the work they perform.

An Environment for Growth

Create a library of videotapes, audiotapes, books, CD-ROMs, workbooks, technical guides, and other materials that employees can use for their personal improvement. Don't be concerned with the loss of these materials when they are being used for performance improvement. They're an inexpensive education and learning alternative. If you have the capability for implementing on-line personal computer or satellite delivery systems within your company, take advantage of the many alternative forms of training that these media make available. Library materials may also be made available through an in-house computer network.

Integrate Employee Growth and Productivity

In some cases, you can integrate your development efforts by having internal experts host technical discussions on the job, during pizza lunches (that the company pays for) or on an "as needed" basis when employees request assistance. You might even establish a rotating coaching role, a person who would be available throughout the day for questions and demonstrations. He or she might "visit" workstations to review and support application of new knowledge or skills on the job, when applicable.

Going Outside the Company

In many areas of the country, there are consortiums of companies that contract for training at reduced rates. Most of the knowledge and skills provided through a consortium are generic, so company specific application issues will need to be supported by the participant's supervisor. Machinery and software suppliers frequently offer training for purchasers of their products. Outsourced providers of training/development will often reduce their rates for long-term contracts and/or partnering arrangements that ensure longevity of the relationship.

Direct Lines of Responsibility

One way to reduce costs and improve the return on your training/development efforts is to have each supervisor/manager work with his or her direct reportees to determine what each individual needs to perform well on the job. The supervisor can then work with each employee to plan for and manage his or her personal development process. Individual development plans that identify the improvement outcome desired and a plan of action specifying what will be done provide support for this process. The use of these plans should be informal rather than formal as in review program atmospheres, or it will appear to be a mandated development program and have difficulty surviving on its own.

Recognition

As you provide for and encourage employee improvement and learning by participating in company sponsored training/development events, remember to deliver special recognition and feedback for those who take advantage of the opportunities. Encourage employees whom you want to retain and groom for future positions to participate in training/development as well. Although you can never guarantee an employee a higher level position, you can provide the opportunity for growth through training, challenging projects, and/or assignments that prepare the employee to be the best candidate for promotional positions when they become available. Explaining this growth benefit helps employees to better understand the reciprocal nature of development and how their initiative and investment of energy is required to prepare for the opportunity.

How Do You Measure the Results of These Training Opportunities?

Tenure of good workers is a good indication of how your efforts are being received. Reduction in turnover is the reciprocal indicator of whether good workers are valuing what you are offering. Retention or work environment survey questions that directly reflect on your training and development efforts are examples of specific feedback that can be measured and tracked over time. Sales and service effectiveness measures are usually maintained and can be used as indicators for specific training conducted to enhance these figures. All the traditional measures of performance in manufacturing such as scrap, cycle time, order fulfillment, and so forth can be used as indicators of training impact. Earnings per employee is a frequently used measure of performance and improvement.

Customer surveys and/or feedback reflect the quality of service received and the satisfaction level that can be improved through focused training efforts. If you have a succession planning process, the measurement might be the readiness lists you maintain to backfill key roles. The number of individuals you have who are ready to fill these roles may be another indicator. A more direct form of measurement is to calculate the return on investment (ROI) from specific training efforts by collecting pre- versus post-performance improvement measures, expenses for creating the training, lost work time, travel, and more.

What Results Can You Expect?

Very few of the suggestions for measurement mentioned previously will show dramatic or immediate changes that can be directly attributed to your training and development efforts alone. But, if the development of people focused on supporting business objectives is a strategy of your organization, the measures of business performance referenced previously will improve over time. You will have developed good people to fill critical performance roles in your organization. You will have effectively re-recruited key contributors who support the achievement of your business objectives. Both your current and future employees will perceive career development as a benefit. A learning environment focused on continuous improvement will assure the ongoing entity status of your organization is maintained.

Good organizations that focus on meeting employees' expectations for career development expect some turnover. But they also expect to keep track of former employees and include them as potential rehires if they should require their knowledge/skills at a future time. These employees are usually willing to return because they know the company values their knowledge and skills and will continue to support their career growth in the future.

The Bottom Line: If You Train Them, They Will Stay

Your employees will make or break your business. One of the higher priorities of the current workforce is to expand its knowledge and skills to remain personally employable in this fast changing business environment. It is the current form of job security for them—-lifetime employability.

Businesses Have a Choice

Make a strategic decision to adjust internal systems and support the employees' requests for career development to engender the corresponding allegiance and tenure which will develop, or choose to ignore employees' career development needs and continue to suffer in a performance system that ensures high turnover rates and lowered productivity. The choice is obvious: if you create an environment which is productive for both you *and* your employees, your productivity will rise and your company will enjoy greater success. Start building for your company's future today.

From Chad Cook's discussion of educational and training opportunities within the company, we move to Brian Grossman for a look at how to deal most effectively with underachievers. As the market for new employees grows tighter and tighter, it makes more sense to retrain and rebuild underachieving employees rather than seek replacements. After all, these employees already understand some of your corporate culture and ideals, whereas you would have to begin the process anew with new hires—if you were lucky enough to find them. Grossman, an expert in career education and workplace psychology, details ways to assist specific types of underachievers in the corporate climate.

12

Building and Holding Underachievers

Brian Grossman, Ph.D.

Most of us have some employees who simply do not consistently apply effort and who are working far below their potential. Their problem is not ability, but attitude. They deny that what they do now has any impact on tomorrow. They are Underachievers.

In the past, when we did not have labor shortages to contend with, we would most often make some attempt to work with those persons. When that attempt failed, and it usually did, we would just let those people go. Not so anymore. We need every employee we can recruit and then some. We can't afford to let people go anymore.

The Center for Applied Motivation is founded upon the understanding that a person's level of achievement is more a result of personality development than level of natural ability. Although each individual is unique, there are four developmental levels of underachievement. These categories are not mutually exclusive, and are often overlapping. So how can you tell if an individual is an underachiever?

Underachievers have the ability to do substantially better work than they are doing, but they lack certain basic attributes:

The ability to work to completion. Underachievers start things well, then lose interest, even in things they say they want.

The ability to function independently. When underachievers are closely supervised they can do very good work, but when the supervision stops, so do their efforts.

The ability to produce within time limits. If classic underachievers are told "Have that project done by Friday," on Friday they are likely to say, "I thought you meant *next* Friday."

These categories are not mutually exclusive. The key to working with an underachieving employee is the application of consistent supervision, training, and effort.

Achievement Profile

The classic profile for the typical underachiever includes characteristics such as:

- Does well on achievement or intelligence tests, but grades fall short of abilities
- Misses deadlines, is late in keeping time limits
- Can do well, but is erratic; needs constant supervision; is not a self-starter
- Seldom accepts responsibility for personal failure: tends to blame "bad luck" or other people

- Starts enthusiastically but quickly fades, promises he or she "will do better next time"
- Appears easily distracted when needing to do work
- Does not respond to punishment, rewards, logic, tutoring, or just being left alone

Most people show some aspects of underachieving at various times. An Underachiever has a pattern of underachieving.

Program Helps Self-Motivation

The training program used by The Center for Applied Motivation is designed to develop and enhance *self*-motivation. Lack of motivation causes underachievement, which leads to a downward spiral of low productivity, acceptance of mediocrity, unhappiness, and failure.

The focus is on motivation, not merely academic issues. Attitude change is our first concern. We have found that until a person has a self-motivating attitude, external approaches (such as tutoring, study skills, logic, and power approaches) are ineffective in maintaining motivation.

The Distant Underachiever

This employee may appear as negative, cynical, a loner, superficial, and feels out of the mainstream. This type of employee will sit alone in the staff cafeteria and avoid social contact. Distant underachievers have difficulty with issues of trust and certainty.

Primarily, distant underachievers are withdrawn from social interaction, preferring instead to focus on solitary pursuit. Any change in their closely controlled environment is often seen as a threat.

The distant underachiever can be a good employee but generally only in a selected area. Often he or she has an advanced vocabulary and technical knowledge as well as abilities for philosophical and analytical discussion. The life of the distant underachiever has repeated anxiety followed by distancing from that which brought on the anxiety. This sequence of events may lead to social isolation, premature job transitions, and short-term relationships.

The distant underachiever approaches relationships that cannot be avoided erratically and impulsively. Often this individual will have great difficulty productively expressing himself or herself. If threatened, he or she will react with hostility and without concern for consequences.

The distant underachiever must be carefully approached in a consistent manner. Even small inconsistencies can undermine the fragile trust and cause a greater distancing. Schedule short but frequent periods of time with this type of employee, being sure to be consistent, on time, and non-threatening.

The Passive Underachiever

The passive underachiever focuses on the acceptance and approval of others without consideration for his or her own needs. All activities and tasks center on the desire of the passive underachiever to gain the approval of authority figures.

The passive underachiever is trying to achieve for others, not himself or herself. Because his or her own needs are not in focus, he or she is constantly pressured by what he or she believes others may want. Anxiety is high, sometimes overwhelming.

The passive underachiever will often respond with ambivalence to the responsibilities of personal relationships and future opportunities. Even for the more positive person, who shows some enthusiasm in performance, consistency in self-motivation is lacking.

The passive underachiever tends to fall within one of four subcategories:

Compulsive: The compulsive passive underachiever focuses on the necessity of order and neatness. This compulsion for order can be seen in the attention to detail that precedes most activities. Room temperature, lighting, even the arrangement of the items on the desk are vital prerequisites for beginning work.

Obsessive: This type of underachiever cannot make a commitment to a task or goal. Instead, they put so much effort into deciding what to do and how to do it that the task itself does not get done. This obsessive underachiever often falls victim to stress-related physical disorders.

Somatic: This type of underachiever, on the other hand, is most likely to use physical distress as an excuse to escape rejection or disapproval. This tendency will become apparent often when faced with situations such as a project deadline, confrontation with a co-worker, or discussion with a supervisor.

Hysterical: This type of underachiever focuses on the acceptance and the approval of the external self. These individuals are controlled by the prevailing trend, in whatever form it may take. This type of individual is a follower, easily influenced by others. The potential for close relationships is limited by narcissistic perceptions.

Working with the passive underachieving employee requires teaching a sense of independence. They need to understand that the goal is not perfection, but consistent effort is required.

The Dependent Underachiever

Dependent underachievers are the most common. They fail to prioritize effectively, often focusing on activities that have little long-term value while ignoring valuable experiences necessary to improve future performance.

Dependent underachievers often focus on nonessential tasks such as sharpening pencils, organizing the desktop, and ensuring paper is in the copy machine. They have difficulty prioritizing their time and experience difficulty in asking for help. When asked about their inconsistent levels of performance they will blame others or events. Their explanations serve to deny them control over their circumstances.

Socially, dependent underachievers are charming and active. Their attitudes toward authority are often ambivalent. Superficially, they respond with indifference, generally withdrawing from authority figures.

Dependent underachievers express anger through passive-aggressive behavior that allows them to view themselves as controlling responses over authority figures. They often use clever excuses to justify their underachievement, hoping that this will focus attention away from them.

They feel that through inconsistent and marginal performance they will become the focus of attention. Therefore, consistent success would destroy the dependent relationship between the underachiever and his or her employer.

To effectively influence dependent underachievers, authority figures must realize that underachievement ultimately is the responsibility of the underachievers. As long as others continue to overly concern themselves with the lack of performance, the dependent underachievers will not be concerned. Only when others are able to place responsibility and consequences back onto the underachievers will they choose to change.

The Defiant Underachiever

Most apparent in late adolescence, and rooted in their insecure sense of self, the defiant underachiever's conflict is between independence and dependence. The adolescent defiant underachiever is just beginning to see himself or herself as an individual separate from the adult world. He or she has not solidified his or her sense of self. Striving to find what role to play, he or she needs unencumbered individual success. Criticism or other suggestions to improve performance result in distance, defensiveness, and oppositional behavior. The defiant underachiever develops difficulties when he or she is unable to easily achieve personal goals.

Regardless of personal preference, the defiant underachiever will frequently, arbitrarily take opposing stances to the opinions and values of the "adult" world.

To avoid failure, he or she will often refer to the "oppression" of authority figures as a rationale for underachieving. However, this type of individual will actually provoke such "oppressive" behavior by authority figures to ensure the continuance of his or her rationalization of underachievement.

Examples of defiant underachiever behavior include:

- Continually arriving late and leaving early
- Turning in projects that are incomplete
- Having other staff minimally angered by their behavior

The defiant underachiever's oppositional behavior continues inflammatorily for all concerned. They are often energetic, creative, open, and aware, but they deny reality. The defiant underachiever's goals should be

- to develop the ability to effectively relate with others
- to grow a stronger self-image to stop the cycle of underachieving

No matter which type of underachiever you're dealing with, it's vital to remember that the lack of achievement is a matter of personality development. Help the individual to grow and you will have a more productive employee.

For More Information

The Center for Applied Motivation has developed a test that can be administered on behalf of an employee to help determine if the employee fits the profile of one of the types of underachievers. For information about the test, please contact The Workforce Stability Institute.

Your front-line workers are the heart and soul of your business. Just as we learned that you must find person and situation specific ways to motivate underachievers, you must also utilize specialized means of motivating and encouraging your front-line people. These are the people who physically allow you to do what you do. Marion Smalle, a Greensboro, North Carolina-based management consultant, explores the ways in which front-line workers can become dissatisfied and offers ideas for how to keep your people happy and working hard. She suggests ways to offer training and education programs, and details incentive programs which go beyond simple pay raise structures.

13

Inspiring Front-Line Workers

Marion Smalle, Ph.D., LL.B.

Employees, particularly front-line employees, are the heart of your business. It seems simple enough to suggest that a company with happy employees is a more productive and profitable company, but the means to making those employees happy are sometimes not as simple as one might think. In an ever more fragmented and mobile job market, motivating, training, and keeping your front-line employees can mean the difference between survival and failure in the new corporate age.

Your front-line workers are the ones with their hands in the soup, so to speak, and it is certainly essential to retain them. However, in order to understand how to inspire these vital cogs, one must first understand their wants and needs.

What Makes Employees Dissatisfied?

When employees, especially in the manufacturing environment, may leave their jobs for as little as 25 cents per hour more, the problem is usually not money, but the way they feel about their value and role in the organization. Furthermore, when 70 percent of employees during exit interviews claim "personal" reasons for their decisions to leave, we should know there is something wrong. In some organizations, a large number of employees refuse exit interviews, and in the most severe cases, don't even collect their final paycheck. Instead, they might send some friend or relative to collect it in order to avoid having to answer any questions about their decision to leave the organization. Why does this happen?

There are two fundamental reasons why people leave their jobs—lack of respect and lack of trust. The jobs front-line people perform are sometimes viewed as "menial" and "routine," and these workers may believe that management finds it difficult to show respect for the people who perform them. Employees begin to feel unimportant and devalued, and often do not understand how their jobs impact the bottom line of the organization. They cannot see themselves in the role of making a contribution to the organization. This crucial gap in communication—the disconnection between management who are the leaders of the organization and the employees who may well be performing the most critical jobs—can be fatal.

Where Do the Breakdowns in Communication Occur?

Employees have a strong need to know what is happening in the organization, and how changes will affect them. Management is often blamed for not "communicating" with the employees, and many employees feel resentment toward management for not informing them about how the company is doing, what the plans are, why certain changes are necessary, how decisions will impact on them, and so on. Although many organizations take pride in communicating regularly with their employees, one has to ask, "What do they talk about?"

Well, that's an interesting question. One CEO proudly stated that he had excellent communication in his company, and that the company's annual and financial statements as well as business plans are posted on the notice board where everyone can see them. Yet, the company was experiencing a 39 percent employee turnover per annum.

Why should the turnover be so high when organizations provide information such as in the example mentioned above? One cannot blame management for feeling a little exasperated when they really feel they are communicating, but employees still claim they are being kept in the dark. The problem is one of method, language, and assumptions about what employees know. Just because a report is posted on a bulletin board doesn't mean that anyone is reading it. Consider how many billboards and advertisements pass through your hands every day without your reading them.

Assuming that employees understand the financial aspects of the marketplace as well as management might also be a false supposition. A recent survey showed that a whopping 49 percent of adults do not understand basic economics. Organizations, therefore, may claim they make public the revenue figures, market share percentages, and other related information, yet in the "real world" manufacturing environment, employees often believe income to be the same as profit. Therefore, they believe the company makes lots of money. For instance, they might not understand cost control in the face of competition, despite the organization's "communication." So, distribution of complicated financial reports to the notice board is, in most cases, a waste of time. At worst, they create confusion and further misunderstandings, and even at best, these postings are highly impersonal.

How Can Communication Errors Be Solved?

Sometimes it's not even as simple as breaking down communication barriers. Front-line employees must feel valued. They must feel necessary. And they must feel as though they are a part of the organization, not just a piece of machinery.

What is required is not paying higher wages. People deserve fair compensation, but a few cents an hour more is not going to change the way people feel about their jobs. It could be argued that it would be hard to find an individual at any level of the organization who feels he or she is being paid enough. Instead, education about how the business really works is what is required. And that education needs to be coupled with emphasizing how the employee contributes and benefits from his or her own performance. Front-line employees understand their jobs only as they have been defined—clock in on time, make the rate on the job, make scheduled production, and hang out in the break area until it's time to clock out. Always look busy in case the supervisor is watching and generally, follow the rules. In short: make sure it looks like "they know the drill."

However, when people can see the "big picture," and how they fit into it, they are more apt to take ownership and responsibility for the outcomes of the organization. If they understand not just "how" to do the job, but "why" it needs to be done, there will be a dramatic increase in their production and commitment to their jobs and their organization. In other words, employees need to feel that they *are* the business, that they *do* make a contribution, and that they are important to the success and longevity of the organization. Understanding and accepting their importance provide the most compelling reasons to stay.

Where Do the Problems Lie?

Many organizations are reluctant to invest in the education of their front-line employees. It is easier for the organization to make the decision to purchase a $5 million machine that is touted to be the best piece of equipment since the electric toaster, than it is to spend a few thousand dollars on employee education. It is ironic, then, when the new state-of-the-art machine arrives, employees are expected to be excited about it, too! It is still the employees, not the equipment, that will make the organization a winning one. Remember that machines will always be just that—machines.

What Happens When an Organization Commits to This Education and Training?

Just like front-line employees, the organization will be faced with countless questions as it embarks upon this new course of action. What should this education involve? What will the outcomes be? How do we measure the results? These are all fine questions when talking about employee education. The good news is, the answers are not rocket science. They are relatively simple.

First, it is not necessary to have employees attend week-long workshops. Do not be scared away by visions of empty offices and million-dollar education and seminar bills. In essence, one day per employee, with sessions of 15-20 participants, should be ample to explain basic business concepts and change the way employees feel about their jobs and the company.

The instruction should be simple and fun, making use of everyday language and examples. You want employees to understand the business and their role in it, not prepare them for a degree in business economics. You also want them to enjoy what they're doing and view the experience as a valuable one.

The choice of facilitator is crucial. Most organizations opt for an outsider to facilitate, for the simple reason that "a prophet is never honored in his own city," and frequently, in-house facilitators are viewed with suspicion. Employees usually feel that the in-house facilitator is a management "goon" and that the organization has ulterior motives. Often employees will claim the sessions are an attempt by management to "brainwash" them. Whichever route the organization decides to take, the facilitator must be experienced in working with front-line employees, and possess strong facilitation skills. These sessions are very demanding for the facilitator.

What Should the Company Look to Gain from These Training Sessions?

Each company should develop its own set of objectives dependent upon the type of business and the level of education required. However, there are some basic goals each company could look to accomplish in any arena.

Employees need to understand:

- How the company operates
- How the company structure works, and how workers fit into that structure
- The concepts of income, expenditure, and profit
- The impact individual actions have on the bottom line of the organization
- The customer/value/profit relationship
- The role of management/self/customer/supplier

Each employee should gain:

- A realization of the individual's own importance and value

- The ability to act in his or her genuine self-interest
- Better long-term prospects
- Teamwork and collaboration between management and front line
- High level of personal motivation

The outcomes for the organization include:

- Increased productivity
- Teamwork and loyalty
- Improved cost control
- Reduced waste
- Enhanced quality
- Reduced absenteeism and turnover
- Increased profits

How Can the Company Measure Success?

Results are easy to measure in terms of production outputs, quality improvements, and employee absenteeism and turnover—the physical aspects of the job. The "intangible" results are often astounding—the obvious increase in motivation and improved attitudes and commitment are what a lot of organizations find to be the most compelling results. Often, people leave the training surprised to know that their input is important to the success of the organization, no matter how "small" the job is. They also understand it is their duty and responsibility to look for ways to do things better, not just for the company, but also for their own future with the company.

Organizations that have invested in this type of education usually state that the ownership result is, by far, the most valuable outcome of this type of education. What's even more valuable are the reports of the lasting results they experience. Even two and three years after the training, organizations are still reaping the benefits. They insist that new hires go through such a program as soon as possible after they join the organization.

That's All It Takes to Keep Front-Line Employees Happy?

Of course, there are many factors beyond education and training that keep your employees happy and productive. Other chapters in this book deal with leadership, hiring, recruiting, recognition, and other retention methods. However, the value of training and business specific education cannot be overlooked, in terms of inspiring and motivating front-line employees.

Despite new technology, innovations, and flavor-of-the-month fads, it is still the *people* who make the difference between a winning company and a losing company. Irrespective of the asset value of an organization, it is only people that can make the difference.

What makes one organization, and not another, a compelling place to work? When employees feel they have purpose and value, when the environment supports ideas and innovation, and when there is collaboration and teamwork between employees and management, employees will choose one work environment over another—and they won't leave your company in search of a better place to work. When employees shift to positive attitudes about their jobs and their company, their behaviors change. They feel a strong desire to help *their* company succeed; therefore, they tend to remain with the organization.

Keep in mind that it is fundamental—both for management and front-line workers—to remember that the company's product is just that—a product. The real heart and soul of any business is its people.

In the coming chapter, Joyce Gioia returns to expand upon Marion Smalle's ideas for motivating front-line workers. She takes the ideas of internal motivation and marketing and applies them to the entire employee community. She presents the concept of viewing your employees as internal customers, just as you view those persons and organizations to whom you market your products as external customers. As such, she suggests means and strategies for marketing to these internal customers, from compensation packages providing value-added services such as childcare and even on-site pet care to bettering internal communications with better copywriting.

14

Internal Marketing

Joyce Gioia, M.B.A., CMC

Bonding with Employees as Valued Customers

Remember how different life used to be, when there was a surplus of employees? People actually *wanted* to work for you and you could pick and choose between applicants. The days of employee surpluses are gone—for the foreseeable future: ten, perhaps fifteen years, perhaps even more? And in order to have the employees we need to get the job done, we have had to change our ways of relating to workers, haven't we? "My-way-or-the-highway," the prevailing corporate culture of the 1960's, 1970's, and 1980's has given way to a more employee-centered one, a culture that we called in our book, "lean and meaningful."

This new lean and meaningful culture is characterized by a focus on the employees of the organization—the human resources—giving them the attention and credit the times demand. These changed times call for a new way of relating with workers. We call that new way of relating *internal marketing*.

Internal marketing takes the same strategies and tactics that companies have used for ages to attract, optimize, and hold onto good customers and recasts them to attract, optimize, and hold onto the organization's *internal* customers, its employees. Internal marketing values the employees, their opinions, their ideas, and their accomplishments in new and acknowledging ways.

Similar to its external cousin, the overriding concept of internal marketing is to add so much value to being part of the organization that the workers would not even consider leaving. They would have to be crazy! The physical, emotional, and psychic rewards are so great that departure becomes the last thing on their minds. And when competitors approach them, as will inevitably happen, they will dismiss those overtures out of hand. So the question is: how do you get to the point where employees feel that way about your company? The simple answer is this: practice internal marketing in every interaction with employees.

Internal Marketing Touches All Aspects of Human Resources

From recruiting to exit interviews, the concept of internal marketing touches all aspects of human resources. It needs to run as a consistent thread, a leit motif, if you will, throughout all the people-oriented activities of the organization. It's easy to understand why you would want to have the principles of internal marketing in the recruiting process; it's not so logical that you would need to keep the principles in mind when you're losing an employee. (We'll explain "why" later.)

The bottom line is that there needs to be congruence in *all* of your activities. From external marketing to internal marketing, from your value-added programs in sales to your dealings with alumni who have left your employ, the messages have to be consistently positive, effective, and aligned with each other. If not, you'll risk generating confusion about your "brand."

The concept of branding in human resources is a relatively new one. Whether you're aware of it or not, every interaction you have with employees and prospective ones establishes and reinforces your brand in their minds. Just as in external marketing, so too is it unwise to confuse your internal consumers with mixed messages. Thus, you'll need to send compatible communications throughout your various expressions. From memos about corporate events to job postings, they all need to have the same connecting thread: "We care about our people."

One of the first corporations to become aware of the importance of branding in human resources has been Sprint Corporation, the telecommunications giant. Sprint takes a holistic approach to all communications across spectrum from internal to external. They leverage their employment brand to be aligned with their strong consumer brand. Sprint believes that their brand reflects their positioning in the marketplaces—both consumer and labor. Their position to consumers is "We help consumers actively shape the world they want." And likewise, their position to employees is closely aligned, "We help our employees shape *their* worlds by providing the opportunities and training that they are looking for." You'll find that position reinforced in *all* of Sprint's advertising, including their employment postings, though 70 percent of their non-entry level positions are filled internally.

Recruiting

The process of retaining employees begins with their first exposure to your company. Ask yourself these questions: What does your recruiting advertising look like? What does it read like? Does it, like most employment advertising, simply tell about "your great company" and what *you're* looking for, or does it talk about what's in it for the applicant, the growth opportunities available with your company? Does it *invite* the prospect, or does the collateral simply say that you're "taking applications"? If your advertising is only talking about your company and what you're looking for, not only will your response be poor, but also the quality of applicants you'll attract will be folks who don't feel like they deserve the best opportunities.

Writing employment advertising should be like writing copy to sell a product or service. You need to tell people "what's in it for them" and you must "sell the benefits." We don't simply mean the employee benefits, as in compensation and benefits. But rather, what are *all* the reasons an applicant should choose your job over the other offers? Do you offer training? Growth opportunities? Free parking? Convenient hours? Flexibility to work around scheduled classes? Fitness facility, daycare, or eldercare on site? Free event tickets? Failure to put any of your benefits in your ads could result in an applicant calling your competitor first.

Where are you displaying your advertising messages? If you're looking to recruit young people and you're not using the web, you're overlooking an extraordinary advertising medium. Young people, savvy and fearless about technology, use the Internet for many of their activities—for entertainment, for communication, for information, and certainly when they're looking for jobs.

How may prospective employees contact you? Last year, I was appalled to see an ad from one of our new clients. The only method offered for response was an on-site application . . . no telephone number, no web site, no e-mail address. Oh, respondents could send résumés—but for warehouse positions, which was the case here, résumés are unlikely.

The more ways you give people to respond, the more responses you'll get. Give them lots of options: e-mail, "snail mail," web site, facsimile, and telephone. Different candidates will choose different media. That's okay. Give them choices.

Hiring

What's it like for a prospective employee to come to your facility for an interview? Do you welcome them as if you are truly happy to see them? Do you make it easy for applicants to complete applications? Do you offer a clean, well-lit area with a table, desk, or clipboard? Once the applications are complete, do you interview the applicants right away or leave them waiting? Your highly valuing their time sends a clear message that they will be respected and valued as employees as well.

During the interview itself, do you give them the third degree, or do you express an interest in *them* and their desire to grow? The interview is your opportunity to pique their interest about your company, find out how *their* goals and aspirations dovetail with the objectives of the company, and let them know what a great place to work you offer. And don't forget the tour of the facility as part of the interviewing process. It's yet another expression of your respect and value for the applicants.

Orientation

One of the most overlooked and important chances for bonding takes place at orientation. Orientation is your golden opportunity to remind your new hires that they made the right decisions in choosing your offers. Orientation is also a great time to let new workers know how much you value their contributions, and to let them know how important their work will be in the grand scheme of things.

Orientation is also your time to communicate your culture through presentations by employees who have successfully risen through the ranks and executives who can credibly talk about the mission and vision of the organization. These presentations will demonstrate achievable career pathing, as well as clearly and concretely communicate that your company believes in supporting employees' growth. (For more information on the Institute's model, see chapter 9, "Orientation and Bonding.")

Internal Communications

From newsletters and house organs to memos about corporate events and notices of job openings, virtually *all* internal communications should be employee-centered. Like the employment advertising that promotes the benefits of working for your company, all of your internal communications must be written with the employees in mind.

After all, *everyone* listens to the same radio station, WII-FM, What's In It For Me? And related to that concept is MMFI, Make Me Feel Important. People love to see their names and photographs in print or posted on the web, for that matter. Enlightened employers comprehend the power of recognizing their employees in newsletters and on web sites.

Corporate events can be another opportunity to recognize your employees' service. In your announcement of the events, don't pass up the chance to acknowledge the committee that is working so hard to make the occasion a success. Put their names right on the announcement. Printing their names on the announcements is simply another small way of saying "thank you" for all of their effort.

Internal job postings should be written in a similar manner to employment advertising, keeping the benefits—as well as the features—in mind. However, be aware that when writing this form of internal communication, you may use any acronyms that are common within the organization with impunity—not wise, if you are writing for external consumption.

Exit Interviews— Your Last Chance to Bond

You certainly may wonder why we are suggesting that you stay employee-centered during exit interviews. Here are two very good reasons: First, workers may be what we call *boomerang employees*. Boomerang employees are those that leave, only to discover that the grass that looked so green on the other side was actually crab grass. Needless to say, they want to come back and we want them back. If the exit interview was handled well, you probably have a good shot at getting them back. If it was not, good luck!

In these challenging times, with labor shortages the rule as opposed to the exception, you can't afford to turn off employees who served you well. You *want* those employees to think well of your company—perhaps even recommend their friends and relatives to work there, even if they themselves no longer do.

There are all kinds of reasons that employees leave one job and go to another. Spouses get transferred. Commuting options change. Sometimes, employees grow beyond the particular opportunities that your company can offer at the time. That doesn't mean you should not support their growth, even if it means they're leaving your employ. If working for your company was a great experience, they will surely want to return when you have the right position for them open in the future. But the exit interview must be handled well, or they will be less likely to want to return.

Some of the more enlightened companies, notably J.P. Morgan, even have alumni associations of people who used to work for their company. The company sponsors annual events for their former employees. Other companies even invite the former employees to join in celebrations with their current employees. And guess what happens? Not surprisingly, some of those former employees choose to return to their previous employers. Does it pay to invest in your former employees this way? You bet it does!

Aligning Compensation and Benefits

The more forward thinking companies have already discovered that when it comes to employee benefits, one size does *not* fit all. That's why the more employee-centered companies have moved in the direction of cafeteria-style benefits programs. The value of different kinds of insurance and services changes as people move through different stages of their lives. By offering a design-it-yourself program, you allow your employees to choose those benefits that have the highest perceived value *to them*, and therefore, you maximize their levels of satisfaction—without spending more money.

Employee Services

No chapter on internal marketing would be complete without a discussion of employee services. As discussed in our book *Lean & Meaningful: A New Culture for Corporate America*, no employee-centered company is complete with offering the services that help workers lead balanced lives. These offerings are part of creating what we call "meaningful work." The type and variety of services should be a reflection of the corporate culture and the employee population. Young employees without children will appreciate on-site pet care and fitness facilities much more than they will appreciate childcare vision discounts.

The currency in today's corporate environment is time, not money. If you can find ways to be flexible and provide your employees with convenient services, you will be more successful than your competition in attracting and holding top talent. The kinds of employee services workers value are dry cleaning, laundry, childcare, eldercare, pet care, fitness facilities, and health screenings. Recreational amenities are also high on employees' lists.

To meet the needs of employees looking for work-life balance and convenience, a new type of organization is emerging. Providing Employer-Sponsored Value Plans (ESVPs), for instance, EmployeeSavings.com consolidates discrete discount offers of goods and services for large employee populations. These offers are made at company specific, customized Web sites.

Eleven categories of products, from groceries to golf clubs, from emergency daycare to mortgages, and even homes are available through this valuable program. Employee Savings.com's marketing partners include AT&T Wireless, Dell Computers, ChipShot.com, BMW, BarnesandNoble.com, Alamo, Avis, BabyCenter.com, Disneyland, Universal Studios, Gourmetmarkets.com, Get-a-Way Today, FTD.com, Gear.com, Hickory Farms, Sees Candies, Sharper Image, and Norwest Mortgage. And the best news, for employees and employers alike, is that it doesn't cost a penny to either group. The suppliers of goods and services pay for the privilege of marketing to these large populations.

The Big Picture

In summary, internal marketing involves most aspects of the company, from its internal communications to the image it projects in its employment advertising. And it is important that all communication present a consistent, congruent brand. By these means, the corporation maximizes the efficiency of its investments—in its employees, in recruiting, and in its consumer advertising.

Are you ready to maximize the efficiency of your investments? Enlist the assistance of your advertising agency or consumer marketing people to help you craft effective messages for your employees.

While marketing your company internally is crucial, if you do not recognize and reward your employees' good work at the same time you are selling them on the benefits of working for you, your efforts are wasted. Bob Nelson, a specialist in what it takes to motivate employees, explores ways to recognize your employees beyond the traditional monetary systems. While rewarding your employees financially is crucial, he says, making sure you can provide them with other more intangible rewards is even more important. Nelson looks at ways of keeping your top performing employees happy and proud of their own work.

15

Recognition for Performance and Retention*

Bob Nelson, M.B.A.

Using Rewards and Recognition to Keep Your Most Valued Employees

Employee retention is vital to the success of any organization. Companies devote tremendous resources to attracting and hiring good people, yet they must be just as diligent about retaining them. And, you can't wait until employees are leaving to establish an environment in which they would prefer to stay. To keep your people, effective retention strategies must be created that are based on one common

---

theme—enhancing the bond among the employee, his or her manager, and the organization. An organization enhances this bond by creating a positive working environment that is stimulating and emphasizes an employee's contribution and personal growth. It is sustained through a culture that accommodates employee lifestyles, and encourages motivation, energy, and innovation. Essential in this formula is the role of one's manager—the most important relationship of any at work. Following are key strategies that are working best today to keep and attract organizational talent.

Motivate Employees Through Recognition and Rewards

While it is true that higher salaries offered by other organizations might be a threat to your employee retention efforts, research shows that traditional pay programs are ineffective for motivating high-performing, committed employees. Compensation has become a right—an expected reward for simply coming to work. Companies will lose their most valued employees if they fail to offer them the intangible intrinsic rewards that money cannot buy. Results of a recent survey by the Council of Communication Management confirm this observation. The study found that recognition for a job well done is *the* top motivator of individual performance.

Study after study has shown that what tends to stimulate and encourage top performance, growth, and loyalty is praise and recognition. Employees want to:

- Feel they are making a contribution
- Have a manager who tells them when they do a good job
- Have the respect of peers and colleagues
- Be involved and informed about what's going on in the organization
- Have interesting, challenging work

In fact, the number one reason why employees leave their

jobs today, as reported by Robert Half International, the staffing firm, is that they do not get praise and recognition in their current position.

ASAP Cubed

Although giving effective praise may seem like common sense, a lot of people have never learned how to do it. I suggest an acronym—ASAP cubed—to remember the essential elements of a good praising. That is, praise should be as soon, as sincere, as specific, as personal, as positive, and as proactive as possible.

As soon: Timing is very important when using positive reinforcement, according to extensive research on the topic. You need to give others praise as soon as the achievement is complete or the desired behavior is displayed. You might even interrupt someone who's in a meeting to provide a quick word of praise until you are able to discuss the achievement with them at greater length.

As sincere: Words alone can fall flat if you are not sincere in why you are praising someone. You need to praise because you are truly appreciative and excited about the other person's success. Otherwise, it may come across as a manipulative tactic—something you are doing only when you want an employee to work late, for example.

As specific: Avoid generalities in favor of details of the achievement. "You really turned that angry customer around—you let him unload all his emotions and then focused on what you could do for him, not what you could not do for him." Specifics give credibility to your praising and also serve a practical purpose of stating exactly what is good about the behavior or achievement.

As personal: A key to conveying your message is praising in person, face-to-face. This praise sends the message that the activity is important enough to you to put aside everything else and just focus on the other person. Since we all have limited time, those things you do personally indicate that they have a higher value to you.

As positive—Too many managers undercut praise with a concluding note of criticism. When you say something such as "You did a great job on this report, but there were quite a few typos," the "but" becomes a verbal erasure of all that came before. Save the corrective feedback for the next similar assignment.

As proactive: Most of us need to invest more time and effort to praise more frequently. Look for opportunities to praise whenever there is positive news such as in staff meetings. Use praising tools such as thank you note cards, voicemail, e-mail, or reminder notes on your planning calendar. Lead with the positive and catch people doing things right. Otherwise you will tend to be reactive and focus primarily on the negative (mistakes and deficiencies) in your interactions with others.

Means of Recognition

Things that are the most motivating to employees tend to be relatively easy to do and cost the least. When it comes to rewards, most managers feel that the only thing their employees want is more money. While money can be an important way of letting employees know their worth to the organization, it tends not to be a sustaining motivational factor to most individuals. Salary raises are nice, but seldom are they what motivates people to do their best on the job.

According to a study of potential workplace motivators by Dr. Gerald Graham, professor of management at Wichita State University, three of the top five incentives ranked by employees were seldom done by employees' managers, even though they had no cost.

For a job well done, a manager could give

1. A personal thank you
2. A written thank you
3. Public praise

When these forms of recognition are performed in a timely, sincere, and specific manner, employees feel valued and appreciated.

Most companies also overlook the power and possibilities of no-cost recognition and rewards. Many of the following methods can also be exercised within the context of most every job in the workplace.

Be Creative with Rewards and Recognition

To be most effective, managers should provide recognition and rewards that are frequent, personal, and creative. When an employee has put in extra effort on a key project or achieved a mutually set goal, managers should recognize the achievement immediately in a unique and memorable way. The more creative and unique the reward, the more fun it will be for the employee, managers, and others in the organization. Friends, family, and co-workers will get to hear about the individual's achievement and what the company did to celebrate it, and the employee will get to relive the recognition many times.

One example of a creative reward is the Omni Service Champions program of Omni Hotels. This program recognizes employees who go out of their way to deliver extraordinary service to customers. Employees are awarded a variety of non-cash incentives, such as medals, ribbon pins for their uniforms, dinner, recognition in the company's newspaper, on posters in each hotel, and, finally, a three-day celebration at an Omni chosen by company executives. Ultimately, the program does award cash prizes to the three highest achievers, but again, money is not the sole motivating factor. The awards, incidentally, are presented at a company gala that all service champions attend.

At the Inter-Continental Hilton Head hotel in South Carolina, an Employee of the Month is selected based on guest questionnaires that evaluate service, with comments by managers playing a role in the selection as well. Those honored receive a plaque, a preferred parking space, lunch with the general manager, and a stay in a suite with complementary meals and beverages.

At Park Lane Hotels International, based in San Francisco, guests were asked to nominate hotel workers who provided outstanding service. The company rewarded all nominees with Sony Watchman televisions and held a grand prize drawing for a twenty-inch television; the guest who nominated the grand-prize winner received two free nights at the hotel.

Reap the Symbolic Value of Formal Awards

The recognition value—that is, the intangible, symbolic, and emotional value of any award—is by far the most motivating aspect for employees. Formal awards are useful for acknowledging significant accomplishments, especially if they span a long period. They can also lend credibility to more spontaneous, informal rewards used regularly by management.

It must be noted that recognizing employees with money, merchandise, or plaques to motivate them can have negative effects. When emphasis is placed on the award, rather than the performance, employees are often given the wrong signal. Cecil Hill, corporate manager of improvement programs at Hughes Aircraft Company, claims, "I have found that certain aspects of the cash awards approach would be counterproductive at Hughes Aircraft. For example, cash awards would reduce teamwork as employees concentrated primarily on individual cash gains. We have also found instances where 'pay' for certain types of intellectual performance tends to denigrate the performance."

To get the most out of formal awards, and to make sure

that the focus of the award remains on the performance and achievement—not the award itself—managers must be skilled in how they present such awards. Here are some ways to maximize the benefits of formal awards.

Present Awards in a Public Forum

Awards are not meant to be presented in the privacy of an employee's office. Schedule a special meeting for the occasion to place an employee "in the limelight." Besides honoring the individual who performed well, recognition is also a message to other employees about the type of performance that gets noticed in an organization. According to management consultant Rosabeth Moss Kanter, "To the rest of the organization, recognition creates role models—heroes—and communicates the standards: These are the kinds of things that constitute great performance around here."

Provide a Context for the Recognition

Managers must provide a context for the achievement and explain how it ties to the larger objectives of the organization. Will this achievement translate into a new product line, more appreciative clients, ongoing cost savings, or other significant goals? How will the achievement potentially impact the overall success of the organization and each person in it? Providing a broader context adds significance to the achievement and to the person being honored.

Share Your Feelings

When presenting an award, emphasize your personal feelings about the achievement or the individual who has achieved. Comments such as "I was excited by your success," or "I'm proud that you are part of my team," give energy to the presentation. If your positive feelings are honest and sincere, they add power to the moment that everyone can feel.

Putting It All Together

Retaining employees today is harder than ever. Skilled workers are—and will continue to be—the most important asset of any organization. They will be in high demand during all stages of the economic cycle. Organizations must realize this reality and reward and recognize employees' achievements on an ongoing basis. Employees must know that if they work hard, their efforts will be appreciated and valued. Successful companies were founded on this belief—and it is on this belief that they will survive and thrive.

Sometimes, even though you believe you have the best training, recognition, and internal marketing systems in place, your best employees still leave. We turn once more to Roger Herman, who first examines larger trends that may provide insight as to why employees leave. He then outlines specific reasons why individual employees may jump ship and head for greener pastures. Roger concludes with methodologies for retaining your top performers— the people you need.

16

Retaining the People You Want

Roger Herman, CSP, CMC

A significant part of workforce stability is getting the right people to stay with you, once you have them on board. Retention of the right people builds continuity, institutional knowledge, performance standards, and a sense of community. When people are happy with their supervisors, co-workers, the company, and the work they do, they are likely to be more productive as well as more loyal. Everybody wins.

The key factor that influences an employee's longevity is the relationship between the worker and the worker's immediate supervisor—at all levels of the organization. Research shows that people want to work for a good boss and they don't want to work for a bad boss. That statement sounds like a "no-brainer," until you begin to look a little deeper. People have been "forced" to work for bad bosses for years; they didn't have a choice, because there was nowhere else to go. Now that they have choices, workers are no longer tolerating bad bosses. They're leaving.

This clear fact means that leadership training for supervisors can have a substantial impact on employee turnover. That's *leadership* training, not more management training. Today's employees want to be supervised differently than employees were in the past. They want to be *led*. They want to feel more like partners. They no longer want to be micromanaged, closely controlled, or treated like easily replaceable parts in a machine.

To hold people today, it's essential to respect them, invite their participation in problem solving and decision making, give them lots of flexibility and autonomy—with accountability—and provide all the support they need to excel. We call this "leadership," even "servant leadership"—and it works.

Why Good People Leave

To gain a better understanding of why people stay, learn why they leave. There are several ways to gather this important information in your organization. Consider exit interviews, re-recruitment interviews, organizational culture surveys, and entrance interviews.

Exit Interviews

Exit interviews are an old standby, but in most cases they provide very little useful information. These interviews are typically conducted shortly after the employee announces imminent departure or on the last day of work. Emotions are high, there is often a desire not to hurt anyone, and the employee wants to depart smoothly without burning bridges.

A better approach is to conduct the interview two to six weeks after the employee has left. Ask how things are going on the new job—listen for the positive descriptors; they may be good indicators of what enticed the worker to move to the new employer. Ask comparative questions, as well as inquiring about what the interviewee recommends you consider doing differently. Appreciate the fact that the worker may have jumped the fence because the grass looked greener on the other side. The worker may have found crab grass and would welcome an opportunity to return. If you want them back, say so—they just may return!

Re-recruitment Interviews

Re-recruitment interviews can be conducted at any time with current employees. Ask them questions such as why they joined your company and how well those expectations have been met so far. What expectations have not been met? Answers to these questions will give you invaluable insight into what people are looking for—and why they might leave if those expectations are not met.

Organizational Culture Surveys

Organizational culture surveys are a highly effective means of collecting information about how people feel about the organization they work for. Employees can respond using a paper and pencil questionnaire or they can enter their responses on an Internet or intranet form. The information gathered is presented in aggregate form to the company's leadership team for their education, evaluation, and action.

We prefer a survey system that compares responses on two dimensions: what people perceive about the current situation (the typical employee attitude survey) and what they believe the situation should be. Using gap analysis techniques, there is much that can be learned from studying how far apart respondents see their expectations with how they see reality.

Entrance Interviews

Entrance interviews are conducted with new hires, asking them why they left their last job(s). The answers will reveal their potential areas of dissatisfaction, so you can guard against the same sort of conditions encouraging them to leave your employ.

The Five Principal Reasons People Leave

Survey after survey has examined why people leave their jobs for supposedly greener pastures. Workers in a various occupations, industries, and locales give a variety of reasons. The motivations for jumping from one job to another can be grouped into five main categories. The conclusion is that there are five principal reasons that good people leave their jobs.

1. **It doesn't feel good around here.** In most cases, this statement reflects a corporate culture issue. Workers are also concerned with the company's reputation, the physical conditions of comfort, convenience, and safety, and the clarity of the mission.

2. **They wouldn't miss me if I were gone.** Even though leaders do value employees, they don't tell them often enough. If people don't feel important, they're not motivated to stay. No one wants to be a commodity, easily replaced by someone off the street. If they feel they are regarded as expendable, they'll leave for a position where they're appreciated.

3. **I don't get what I need to get my job done.** Contrary to opinions heard all-too-often from management, people really *want* to do a good job. When they're frustrated by too many rules, red tape, incompetent supervisors or co-workers, inadequate tools and equipment, or insufficient information, people look for other places to work. They want to understand what results they're expected to achieve, to have access to the resources they need to get the job done, and finally, they want the freedom to perform.

4. **There's no opportunity for advancement.** No, we're not talking about promotions, although many deserving people would like to move up. The issue here is learning. People want to learn, to sharpen their skills, and to pick up new ones. They want to improve their capacity to perform a wide variety of jobs. Call it career security: it's a marketability issue. The desire is for training and development. If workers can't find the growth opportunities with one company, they'll seek another employer where they can learn.
5. **The compensation doesn't meet my needs.** Workers want fair compensation, but the first four reasons take priority. If they're not well met, but money's high, you'll hear people say "you can't pay me enough to stay here." Even with the first four reasons in mind, there are a lot of employees who feel they can better themselves just by chasing more income.

Research shows that most people shift their loyalties to a new employer because of non-monetary factors. We emphasize this fact because we have heard a great number of business owners, executives, managers, and supervisors express their belief that people "go where the money is." That argument simply isn't totally true anymore. People are hungry for opportunities to grow in their jobs. They crave advancement, both in position and stature, and in responsibility and opportunity. If they can't find avenues for growth in one environment, they'll seek them in another. People want to make a difference, to be involved, and to be sincerely appreciated for their contributions. They want life balance—more time for themselves and their families to enjoy the fruits of their labors.

Employee Retention Strategies

Corporate Culture

People want to feel good about the place they work. The

physical place is important, but so is the culture—the way it "feels" to be there.

Physical factors include accessibility, safety, lighting, heating/ventilation/air conditioning, noise, comfortable furniture, and similar factors. People like windows to the outside, plants, color, and a comfortable sort of environment. It is possible to achieve satisfactory arrangements for the physical surroundings in practically any kind of workplace. Each workplace is different, of course, but each can be designed suitably for what workers in that setting prefer and expect.

The element of culture is another matter. An organization's culture is influenced most strongly by senior leaders—in the way they lead, communicate, interact with their subordinates, and present themselves and their people to the outside world. People are much more comfortable following leaders who know where they're going, why they're headed that way, and how they're going to get there. Strong leaders guide the development—by the employees—of mission, vision, and values statements. These vital statements, which should be examined and changed or confirmed on a regular basis, form the foundation of what the organization is all about. They give employees something to believe in, something to adhere to, something to follow. We'll cover this topic in more depth in the next chapter.

The key is to create and maintain the kind of working environment that inspires people to want to come to work each day. The organization earns a reputation as being a good citizen and a good employer. It's a place where people want to work.

Relationships

While we've emphasized the importance of the relationship with the immediate supervisor, relationships with all fellow employees are important. People want to feel valued, as if they're making a contribution.

People want to be treated with respect. They want to be seen as being integral to the organization's success and recognized for their parts in making positive things happen. When people issues are well addressed by management, employees will demonstrate their loyalty and dedication as team players in spite of the most adverse circumstances. However, when people are not treated well, they won't "invest" themselves in the company even under the best of corporate circumstances.

Encouraging social interaction in the workplace, on a business level, can be very positive. When people can meet for breakfast, coffee, lunch, or just to kick around some ideas, they build relationships that establish emotional bonds among people, their work, their customers, and others. Those emotional bonds make a big difference in how we can hold our people. The emotions in a work relationship—employees connecting with all the various aspects of the work experience—are not dissimilar to the emotions in a marriage. To keep a marriage strong, emotions need to be expressed and reinforced continuously. The same thing applies in the work relationship, but how often do we tell our employees how much we appreciate them? Little things can have a large impact.

It's unrealistic to think that people will be happy with everything management decides or does. Corporate Camelot doesn't really exist. Reality is that some people will differ with management from time to time. Mature people in any organization expect this circumstance. Often the key is not *what* is done, but *how* it is done . . . and explained. Open communication is essential.

Support

Our assumption is that people want to do a good job wherever they are employed. With our full-employment labor market, they have plenty of choices about where they work—so no one is forcing them to stay with any particular employer. After everyone has left for the jobs they want, the people who remain really want to be there. They want to do a good job. They want it to be easy to do a good job.

Red tape, self-serving supervisors, inappropriate policies and procedures, and inadequate equipment and supplies will turn off dedicated workers faster than you can say "workforce stability." They want support to move forward and get results, not obstacles that get in the way of progress.

These results-oriented employees want a clear understanding of their goals and objectives. They want to understand how they're being measured. They want access to information they need to see the big picture as well as the specific jobs they're working to accomplish. An increasing number of companies are moving toward "open book management" to give their people a greater sense of sharing, openness, and partnership.

Whenever they need help to get things done, they want to know that their supervisors—at all levels—will be there for them. They appreciate "servant leadership," the concept that suggests that the leader's role is principally to provide whatever his or her people need to perform. These high-performing employees *want* to excel, so everything that can be done to help them achieve will also inspire them to remain with the employer.

Growth

People want to grow, personally and professionally. To retain them, build a learning environment that encourages and supports that growth. When leaders and managers genuinely believe in education and training, the message comes through loud and clear.

There are a number of things you can do to emphasize a learning environment. Make magazines and journals about your field available to all your employees. Establish a lending library of books, videotapes, audiotapes, and electronic media. Purchase learning materials for your people and participate in discussion groups about what people are discovering. Wherever possible, link these learnings to opportunities to improve performance on the job.

Provide tuition reimbursement for courses taken at community colleges or universities. Bring in professional trainers or use your own internal resources to teach people. Include courses that will help them in their work, as well as those things that are just good to know.

To send a clear message about your dedication to the growth of your people, prepare a learning plan for each one of them. In the personal growth plans, describe what new knowledge or skills might be important for the employees' personal and professional growth over the coming year. For those areas you want to address, list what training and education programs the employees will participate in during the next twelve months. As much as possible, schedule the "whens and wheres" so the employees see you're really serious about this project. Review the plan and your progress every quarter to assure that you and your employees are fulfilling your obligations. Each quarter you can plan another quarter into the future. The employees uncertain about staying with you will see the commitment to their ongoing growth and will remain employed by your organization so they can keep learning.

Compensation

There are several areas of emphasis on compensation in these days of turbulence in the workforce and the workplace. First, it is important to assure workers that they will be fairly compensated in comparison to others in the community with similar competencies. Second, it is essential to provide benefits that are appropriate and *perceived to have value* by those who receive them. Third, and perhaps most crucially, you should concentrate pay plans more on "pay for performance."

As employees become more concerned with managing their own career destiny, they are becoming more receptive to compensation plans that base their monetary rewards on results achieved. Practically every job can be measured in some way, so use those measurements to guide the amount of money people receive for performing the work. The better they perform, the greater their results, the higher their compensation. Bonuses—spontaneous and pre-planned—are gaining popularity these days.

Money is no longer the major motivator that it was even half a generation ago. People do want to be compensated fairly, but they're looking for much more than just a fat wallet. Just saying "thank you" and showing appreciation in other ways—gift certificates to dinner, four movie passes, a letter of commendation (send a copy home)—is part of compensation today.

Send the Message

Your people are your most valuable—and your most volatile—asset. Treat them well. Care about them. Communicate with them. Treat them as partners.

You're sending messages to your employees every day. The way you work with them sends a message. The way you greet them sends a message. The way you carry yourself— your confidence, attitude, "connection" with the heartbeat of the company—all send clear messages. Be consistent and be congruent. Not only will good people stay with you, they'll recruit more good people to join the team.

Roger Herman continues his discussion of the finer points of employee retention in the coming chapter. What are we to do with all of the information presented so far? Herman tells us that all the good information and good intentions in the world will be meaningless without good leadership. He examines new trends in leadership and what employees will want from their leaders.

17

Leadership Makes a Difference

Roger Herman, CSP, CMC

Why Workers Stay or Go

The critical factor that influences whether an employee will stay with an employer is the relationship between the employee and his or her immediate supervisor. This fact is true at all levels of the organizational hierarchy, from the frontline hourly worker to the executive assistant to the chief executive officer. Who the boss is and how the boss operates are increasingly important factors to employees who have a choice about where they work.

Workers want a boss they can respect, but also who respects them. They want leaders who care, who know where they're going, and who know how to lead the organization to the achievement of the desired goals and objectives.

While some may say there is little difference between leadership and management, there really is a significant shift underway in the corporate world. This shift is being caused by changes in what people are looking for from the people they report to. The style of leadership or management in an organization has a powerful influence on how people feel about working there . . . and how motivated they will be to stay with the employer.

Managers may do a fine job coordinating all their resources, following schedules to meet deadlines, and have all the details well in hand. They have things under control, and may even be admired for their efficiency. However, they may not be leaders. Today's employees want to be led more than they want to be managed.

What Is Leadership?

Leadership involves working closely with people. People follow their leaders because they want to, because they have confidence in their leaders to guide them and their organization into the future. People want to believe their leaders know what they're doing and are dedicated to helping people and organizations achieve their goals. Workers want to respect their leaders' knowledge and be proud of them and the way they operate. They want to have confidence that their organization has a bright future—worthy of their staying with the employer for a long time. People want to work for stable organizations with solid futures.

People working for leaders, rather than managers, feel more a part of what's happening because their leaders keep them informed. The sharing of information and ideas is a two-way street, benefiting all concerned. Employees feel a part of what's happening. They experience a special sense of belonging that motivates them to be more dedicated to excelling in the work they do for you and for your organization.

Leaders are sensitive, staying alert for signals about how

things are going in the work group. When problems arise, leaders respond assertively to solve the problems—before they become serious. Leaders listen carefully to their people to gain a full understanding of situations before taking action. Observing this sensitivity, people feel comfortable about communicating necessary information without fear of consequences.

Results-oriented leaders strive for consistency and cooperation. They appreciate that many people need stability and support, and they work consciously to fulfill those needs. They don't make frequent changes that are unsettling to their subordinates. People should be able to rely on their leaders to act in an intelligent, mature manner to help them achieve the desired results.

Organizations that are led by teams of results-oriented leaders have a special kind of corporate spirit. It's not a pep rally kind of spirit. Rather, it's a sort of focus and devotion to getting the right things done, the right way, on time . . . because it's the right thing to do. That kind of spirit builds a pride in achievement—high achievement—that serves as a source of continual motivation and strength. That deep sense of laser-like energy is unconquerably powerful.

The more managers who adopt the principles of results-oriented leadership, the stronger the organization will be. This synergy creates a force of multiple energies, rather than merely the sum of the committed leaders.

The Emerging Leadership Style

The emerging style of leadership today is something we call "facilitative leadership." In this mode, the leader facilitates the high performance of each individual worker. The leader learns about the worker's potential, then helps the worker reach that full potential, then raises the bar and begins the process anew. Each person is growing, accomplishing more than anyone thought possible and feels wonderfully fulfilled. It's a highly individualized process.

The facilitative leader does not manage people. Believing that we manage *things*, but lead *people*, the emphasis is on providing targets, information, inspiration, growth, support, and coaching. While teams are not ignored, the emerging design suggests that, given the opportunity, people will form their own teams. The collaborative relationships that develop are considerably more productive than those achieved by teams that are formed by management decree.

Making It Work

To be an effective facilitative leader, you have to shift your thinking from the traditional patterns that have dominated management for decades. You are no longer a manager; you no longer *tell* people what to do. Quite the contrary, as a facilitative leader, you expect others to manage themselves. It's a totally different dynamic that places the initiative, responsibility, and accountability squarely in the lap of the worker. The employee becomes more a partner than a subordinate. You're working together to achieve the agreed-upon results.

It's important to recognize that while some workers will absolutely love this kind of relationship, others will be horrified at first when they realize that they now have control over their own performance, their own destiny, and often their own rewards. That's scary stuff for people who are accustomed to being told what to do every step of the way. Begin by developing a clear understanding of what your relationship is, so that you will be able to build from there.

The Vision Process

The next step is to create a vision together. This kind of discussion may sound a bit touchy-feely or out there on the edge. It's still a good conversation to have, especially as you initiate this new relationship. Together, look into the future. What does it look like as you work differently than you have in the past? What will you expect from each other in terms of information, coordination, support, communication, confirmation, and appreciation? How will you relate with others outside your work group, particularly if they don't understand your new approach?

Part of the visioning process will be getting comfortable with the new design. Each person has to "get" what it will be like to operate in a substantially different way. An important part of this exploration is a discussion of values. What's important? What shared values will make the new relationship work? When two people—or more—sit down to talk about the values that are vital to success, a surprising congruence emerges.

Values that we often take for granted—quality, customer service, quick response, respect, personal growth, and others—will be accepted by all. In-depth discussion, however, will enable people to more deeply explore what these values really mean and how they will be manifested in the new work design.

Individual participants may bring up values that are important to them. Some may value flexibility, while others may be happier with a more formal environment. Some may place a high value on being able to leave work at a certain time in order to achieve the desired balance with their families. Others may emphasize the use of technology.

As you talk about personal values, why they're important and how they're reflected in what you do and how you do it, you will actually be developing a set of ground rules to govern how you will work with each other.

Lots of "what-ifs" will emerge in these conversations. Many of them will be very positive what-ifs. If we did such-and-such . . . wow! What a difference that could make. You'll be talking about dreams, desires, preferences for the way life would be if you could really take control of the future. Guess what! That's exactly what will be happening. You'll each be creating your dream job, then supporting each other to make those dreams a reality. People will realize that they can develop for themselves just the kind of job they've always wanted. And, as that design becomes real, workers will understand that their search for the ideal job is over. Turnover plummets because there is no longer any reason to leave. Why would someone want to escape from a self-created perfect job?

Focusing the Discussion

Focus will be necessary. It's easy to believe this new relationship is simply *laissez-faire*, with no accountability, results expectation, or consistency. When workers and leaders in a facilitative leadership environment have a clear focus of where they're going and what's expected of them, most of the confusion and ambiguity dissolve. This need for focus helps us understand the value of sharing information, so everyone sees the big picture. It's vitally important to ensure that *everyone* understands where they're going—individually and as a team.

While it's important that people know where they're going—that they have a sense of direction—they also have to know how to measure their progress. Milestones, measurements, goals, and objectives will all help your people know how well they're moving forward toward targeted accomplishments.

With greater knowledge of what's to be done, people are very comfortable assuming personal responsibility for their work. From time to time, especially when they're new to this kind of environment, employees may approach their leader with questions about what should be done or how something should be done. Rather than responding with specific directions, good leaders ask "What do you think?" The ball is put back in the worker's court, with the employee encouraged to find the best answer. Eventually, this process becomes so comfortable that workers become more interdependent than dependent. They all work together to get big things done.

Inspiring Relationships

Inspiration is a key component of the facilitative leadership design. People have to *want* to operate under this new design to make it work. It can't be forced. People have to be excited about what they're doing. Their work has to be meaningful; they must feel inspired to do their work because of the difference they will make in the world around them. Most people no longer want to simply show up for work to perform a job that is boring, meaningless, or seems like a waste of their time and talent.

In a stable work environment, leaders are close to their people. They do not stay in their offices; they're out where things are happening. Their very presence communicates a sense of partnership: a sharing of the work, not a dumping. The continuity that develops in a stable organization supports open, communicative relationships that build a deep sense of comfort among employees. People feel like they belong and there's very little motivation to even consider working somewhere else.

Obviously, the work environment will be highly influential in determining whether people will be attracted to an employer . . . and whether they will stay. The leadership styles of the executives, supervisors—and followers—will foster a stable, positive environment. As the labor market becomes even more competitive, relationships among the people working for an organization will become increasingly important.

What, then, is workforce stability? How can we synthesize all the information provided in this volume? How can you use the tactics and ideas discussed here to improve productivity in your company? Roger Herman and Joyce Gioia return once more to bring it all together.

18

Workforce Stability: Your Competitive Edge

Roger Herman, CSP, CMC
Joyce Gioia, M.B.A., CMC

The New Workforce Requirement

Given today's employment environment, building a stable workforce is serious business. The stability really does give an employer a competitive edge, when other employers are not able to demonstrate the same strength.

Workforce stability means that the employer has depth, continuity, and institutional memory to serve both internal and external customers. This strength practically assures that the company will enjoy higher levels of performance, productivity, and profits. Efficiency and effectiveness will be much greater than in companies with debilitating employee turnover. Morale will be higher; people will *want* to do a good job as they work together as an experienced, proficient team. With stability, essentially everything in the organization will work better, more smoothly, more meaningfully.

All this descriptive wording sounds wonderful, but so what? The "so what" lies in the capacity of the organization to accomplish its goals, to generate the desired return on investment of all sorts of resources. There is a much greater chance that the employees will achieve whatever they set out to do. This feeling of confidence is powerful when an employer seeks to differentiate itself from its competitors.

That differentiation will be increasingly important. Competition is increasing. In our hot economy, there's plenty of business to go around, but aggressive companies are, understandably, eager to capture as much as they can for themselves. In this kind of environment, some employers do very, very well; others flounder, struggling to achieve market penetration and market share. With the evolution of electronic commerce, globalization, consolidations, and intricate strategic alliances, companies will be challenged to do their work well. There will be little room for error; the emphasis will be on performance. But, it takes people to perform. A company with a turbulent work environment with too much employee turnover will be hard-pressed to get results.

Strategic Positioning

From a strategic perspective, competition for business has always been important, and will continue to be central to corporate operations. Strategists are highly sensitive to the messages they send to the world. The more they can convey the image of being strong, stable, and ready to do the work expected of them, the better positioned they will be recognized in the marketplace.

Human resource professionals and people-sensitive executives are now focused on competition, as well. It's a new kind of competition: the competition for competent workers. Without adequate talent on board, it will be practically impossible to triumph over competitors. With the intensifying demand for good people, workers have choices about where they work, how engaged they will be, and how long they'll stay with an employer. Qualified workers are considerably more mobile today, though many of them actually yearn for opportunities to put down some roots for a long tenure of employment. Unfortunately, these dedicated workers are too often turned off by the circumstances they face in most work environments—so they keep searching for that elusive ideal position.

Employers who are successful in attracting, optimizing, and holding good workers will enjoy a competitive advantage. It's a whole new design in corporate strategic positioning that will gain more and more attention as the labor market gets tighter and tighter during the first decade of the 21st century. The issues surrounding stability affect a wide range of aspects of doing business, including the concerns of a number of highly important stakeholders.

Stakeholders

Stability is important to several families of stakeholders. The level of stability—real and transmitted through performance—substantially influences the relationships between the employer and other entities that interface with it. Each of these relationships can be critical to an organization's success. The stronger the performance of a company, the stronger will be the bonds linking it to the vital components of the outside world. The deeper the relationships, the less ambiguity, hesitancy, and uncertainty will inhibit mission fulfillment.

Customers obviously want their suppliers to be stable. They desire long-term relationships with people who know the product or service and its various applications, the industry, and the customers themselves. A sense of history is valuable, especially in environments where there has been a lot of change.

When customers can have the confidence that the people taking care of them know what they're doing, there's considerably less resistance to recommendations and sales presentations. A deeper sense of trust replaces suspicion and doubt. Customers don't harbor the misgivings that may flow from interaction with suppliers they don't know or believe in.

When these strong relationships develop and grow, which takes place over a period of time as people become comfortable with each other, there is little motivation for customers to even consider other suppliers. The long-term commitment to do business together solidifies the supplier's position, even to the point of being able to forecast the flow of orders and payments. This constancy in operations eliminates uncertainty and enables the company to manage its affairs much more efficiently over the long term. Knowing what to expect allows corporate management to operate in ways that drive more dollars to the bottom line.

Suppliers

Suppliers are always concerned about the strength of their customers. When an employer can demonstrate workforce stability to suppliers, credit terms become much more flexible. The supplier knows it can depend on its bills getting paid because the company can get the job done for its customers and will have the money to pay. Suppliers' sales executives prefer dealing with stable companies because the people they call on understand what they're talking about. The salespeople don't have to waste time on every sales call explaining things the customer should already understand.

The increased efficiency of long-term, in-depth relationships frees time for the suppliers' representatives to provide specialized help that gives the company even more of a competitive advantage. Experts sharing with each other can develop better ways to do things, probably increasing the potential return on capital and materials. Suppliers may partner more with stable companies, sharing research and development and giving the company a preferential position in acquiring new technology, products, or market position.

Investors

Investors watch carefully where their funds are at work. If they see a lot of employee turnover, flashing warning lights attract their attention. They question how stable the company is—low retention rates and instability may well suggest that there are deeper problems in the organization. This company might not be such a safe place for investment dollars. When a company's workforce is stable, investors can enjoy a greater confidence that their money is safe . . . and that the company has a greater chance of producing good returns over the long haul.

Employees

Prospective employees are often curious about a company's workforce stability. If a lot of people have been around for a long time, the company is probably a good place to work. They will have experienced workers to turn to when they need answers, advice, or history. People will know what they're doing, the culture will be solid, and turmoil will not inhibit their performance or job satisfaction. When employee turnover is high, however, prospective employees become skittish and suspicious. They wonder, "What's wrong? Maybe this place isn't where I want to be." Competing for quality employees is considerably more difficult when you are recruiting from a base of instability and uncertainty.

Current employees are sensitive to workforce stability. When they see people leaving, they naturally are curious about why co-workers are departing. They begin to question why they're still around and become more receptive to overtures from recruiters from other employers. When a workforce is unstable, current employees spend a lot of time worrying, listening to rumors, and wasting time in other ways that substantially reduce productivity and profits.

The Workforce Stability Model

Achieving stability in an organization's workforce involves much more than just hiring some good people and telling the world that everything is fine. The proof is in the performance. Fancy talk, pretty brochures, and a robust web site simply won't be enough to convince the various groups of stakeholders that your organization is stable. Public relations hype does not make a company's workforce stable. There's a lot more involved.

This book has presented the various elements of the workforce stability model. Each of these elements is important to achieving stability. None of the elements alone will build stability; they all must be addressed in the employer's strategy. Concentrating on one or two elements won't be sufficient.

It's easy to second guess and criticize any model. Our workforce stability model is no exception. There is one piece missing that will raise some eyebrows. We have not included the compensation aspect of workforce stability. This "deficiency" is deliberate.

Our perspective is that compensation is certainly important. The wage and salary issue—how much money workers take home in their paycheck—will always be paramount. Fringe benefits have taken on a higher level of value in recent years, as well. These compensation factors, along with stock options, special perks, and attractive personal deals will continue to be used by employers to lure desired workers.

From what we see in the employment world—now and in the foreseeable future—other forms of compensation will be perceived as being more in the competitive arena. A major example is time off. People are tired of working all the time. Work-life balance will be a stronger factor than more money in the paycheck in the years ahead—it already is for many people responding to surveys about what's important in compensation. Creative benefits such as concierge services, childcare and eldercare, pet care and pet-oriented benefits, wellness programs including workout facilities and trainers, and company-sponsored involvement in community activities are moving into sharper focus.

There are so many variations on the theme of compensation and benefits, it's practically impossible to steer a path through the jungle. Employers will continue to throw money at the problem until they realize that workforce stability is a much bigger issue than just economics. Our contention is that if employers follow the concepts presented in this book, the financial incentives aspects take a lesser position. They'll always be prevalent, but not worthy of a particularly heavy level of attention.

Authenticity

Authenticity is essential in workforce stability. That authenticity comes from employees subscribing to the same beliefs as management. If the workers don't buy into what management says about the organizational culture, career development opportunities, collaborative relationships, and all the other elements of workforce stability, the whole thing is a sham. Stability will not exist in reality, just in the minds of management; people will still leave, regardless of what management says. The philosophies and practices must be genuine.

If employers practice the principles and methodologies presented in the workforce stability model contained in this book, they will establish and maintain a more stable environment. Authentic application of the elements is crucial; playing games with words and numbers will not last long. When stakeholders discover they've been tricked, they will abandon corporate management quickly and permanently. Not being authentic will be significantly more damaging than might be imagined. The values being expressed by employees today make it clear that they will not tolerate insincerity.

When employers honestly and enthusiastically pursue workforce stability, great gains will be seen. The new, improved status may not be seen immediately, but the strength will come much faster than might be expected. The process will seem more rapid because of the relatively slow progress made by organizations that are not focused on building stability and high performance.

The result? Workforce stability will become your competitive edge.

Appendix

Although it does not fit with our Workforce Stability Model, we have included this chapter on Verifying Performance because it is very important for anyone who hires workers. With our litigious society, employers can't be too careful. This chapter is a guide for getting the information you need in order to make an informed decision and avoid hiring mistakes.

Verifying Performance

Wayne Outlaw, CSP, CMC

The Most Untapped Resource to Make Good Hiring Decisions

Thoroughly checking candidates' references and backgrounds is one of the most important, yet the most neglected, steps of the hiring process. An individual's past performance and behavior is the best indication of future job performance. Information obtained from references can give a clear indication of a candidate's job performance and work history. Background checks not only expose problems, but also can help insulate an employer from charges of negligent hiring. In today's litigious society it is essential that employers perform "due diligence" prior to hiring.

Many managers believe or hope that, given a chance or a fresh start, a candidate will dramatically improve job performance in a new job and even make significant, positive changes in conduct. They are optimistic and believe individuals can change. Yet history has shown such a dramatic shift is the exception rather than the rule.

It is an unfortunate fact that employers check references on only about 12 percent of the people they hire. If you doubt this statistic, think about how many requests for references you have received for previous employees. Do you get calls on one out of five, one out of ten, or even less? When potential employers call you, are they only checking recent jobs?

With the evident lack of diligent, thorough reference and background checks, is it any wonder employers often discover a new employee has problems similar to those experienced in previous positions? Before making a hiring decision it is critical to verify the information and impressions gained throughout the hiring process, especially during interviews, by thoroughly checking references with past employers and not just recent ones.

If the new employee is being placed in a position where the company could be legally vulnerable, reference checking *must* be supplemented with background checks for felony convictions, education or credential verification, and possibly credit history. Everyone has heard horror stories about companies that did not do their homework and later an employee engaged in an act causing damage. Because the company did not do their hiring with "due diligence" to discover this problem and protect employees and customers, the company can be held liable.

Even if an employee does not engage in an act for which the company can be held liable, poor job performance can cost the company and the executive responsible for hiring the employee, plenty. We have all heard stories of employees caught embezzling from a company and on investigation it was discovered that the employee embezzled from previous employers as well. This occurrence is more common than you would think because many employers are embarrassed by it and may quietly force the employee to pay restitution or they may terminate him or her. Since 88 percent of potential employers don't check references, the dishonest employee has an excellent chance of victimizing another company by landing another job and repeating the same behavior.

Some employers check references, but don't heed the warnings they uncover because they think things will be different. A client told us about terminating an employee for embezzling a sizable amount of money during a period of several years. After filing criminal charges, the client received a call requesting a job reference for the terminated employee. The client freely explained the charges against the employee and gave details of the situation, which were available in the public record and published in the newspaper. At the end of the conversation, the client asked what the potential employer was going to do. The response was, "She looks like she was a good employee except for the money problem. We're going to hire her, but not let her handle money." Subsequently, the terminated employee was convicted, received a jail sentence of 18 months, and was ordered to pay restitution. Some employers do not heed even the strongest indications of potential problems. In the event "red flags" and even subtle warning signs are not heeded, the employer will be the loser.

References are critical not only to limiting legal liability, but also to reducing turnover and increasing productivity by enabling a better hiring decision. Referencing is not just a means of fending off undesirables, but is an active way to build a higher quality, more productive, and stable work force. Imagine the money saved or profit increased, if you reduced turnover by only two, five, or even 15 percent. If turnover is reduced more, the results are even more dramatic.

Most large organizations are clearly aware of the necessity of checking references, but in small companies or companies with leaner staffs the need is even more critical. If an employer with a few employees makes a mistake in hiring, the impact can be devastating and even cause the company to "go under." The pain and agony of turnover and having to go through the process all over again should be motive enough to make sure references are well checked.

A candidate with bad references rarely develops into a good employee. Most applicants are very skilled at providing names of "good" references. Some are even good at covering up "red flags" or problem situations.

Because of the need to verify backgrounds, especially to protect others in the workplace, the majority of states have passed legislation providing employers with a "qualified privilege" protecting them from liability if they faithfully attempt to give an accurate representation of the employee's past performance. Many companies ask former employees to sign a letter indemnifying them from harm when they are requested by a former employee to provide references. The form can be part of the out processing of a terminated employee. They can elect if they want the former employer to provide a reference.

Reasons for and Frequency of Lying

It appears that lying is so commonplace it is even expected. During the 1992 presidential election campaign, there were so many lies exposed that *Time* magazine [October 5, 1992] ran a cover shot of a person with a wide grin and sunglasses. The caption read, "Lying: everybody's doing it (honest)." The perception of everybody lying has taken the stigma away from telling "white lies," omitting some of the facts, fudging, or making misstatements.

Why do people lie in the first place? Candidates lie, fudge, or make misstatements in order to conceal a shortcoming or a problem, or to gain an unfair advantage. They might lack expertise in a particular area or experience in a specific discipline. They may lie to cover up periods of unemployment, performance problems, or leaving under less than desirable circumstances.

Most lies do not remain secret once the candidate starts working. The employer easily discovers a false claim on the résumé or application, when the employee is asked to perform the skill claimed. The employee either quits in frustration or is fired for incompetence. Even if the employee is a fast learner and can develop the necessary skills, his or her lack of skill or experience will still increase the learning curve and reduce productivity.

Jude M. Werra, president of an executive search firm, says that a significant number of executive level candidates misrepresent academic credentials. To publicize this misrepresentation, he has created a "Liars Index." He has consistently found that almost 15 percent of the candidates for top-level jobs in companies falsify academic credentials. Because these credentials are easily checked, one wonders what else, not so easily checked, is falsified. This level of falsifying academic credentials remains consistent year after year, even when it is published in a well-known publication such as *USA Today.*

To assist companies, the states of Iowa and Kentucky have passed legislation directed at this problem. In these states, people who flagrantly claim a degree or other certification are in violation of the state law. Other states are considering similar laws; however, this legislation will not be enough to protect the employer.

It is important to realize applicants and employers see résumés differently. Employers see a résumé as a precise document that should be entirely factual. Job hunters, however, see a résumé as a marketing tool, and think embellishments are natural and will be forgiven. Many lies are added to a résumé earlier in a career to "get a foot in the door" or enhance the applicant's chance of being hired.

Fear of Providing References

Reference sources, usually employers, are fearful of being sued by applicants for defamation of character and tend to be conservative in giving references. Some companies will provide only name, dates of employment, and job titles. As mentioned earlier, employers in most states are given a "qualified privilege" in providing references for former employees. If the information is factual and can be verified, the company cannot be held liable, except in special cases. If the reference check does not delve into unsupported information or outside the job responsibility and performance, courts generally uphold this "qualified privilege," and the conversation is protected. Facts honestly given or opinions honestly held constitute a solid and reasonable defense against defamation claims.

Begin with the Application

Many large companies have applications that are "legal" but not designed to provide accurate, adequate information for easily checking background and references to verify performance. The application, not the résumé, is the critical document for checking references and not enough care is given to application design and construction. Many smaller employers buy a generic application from an office supply store. These off-the-shelf applications don't ask for complete dates of employment, exact job title and responsibilities, contact information of past employers, reason for leaving, or other key facts. They also do not ask for job specific information. For example, if a position involves using a company vehicle, it is critical that exact information about the individual's driving history—including accidents and tickets—be provided on the application. Generic applications do not consider the position's essential job functions as defined by the Americans with Disabilities Act (ADA).

The company's application should also include a detailed release authorizing the employer to check references. It should also include a Release of Liability indemnifying and agreeing to hold harmless those who will be contacted as references and those contacting them. The signed release goes a long way in protecting the employer from liability. The application is a key legal document and, in the event the company is sued, will be the primary evidence. It should be designed to be legally defensible in case litigation occurs by requesting only the information necessary to determine an applicant's qualification for the position.

Some business owners are reluctant to put the burden on the candidate to provide needed information. This reluctance is a mistake. Always ask the candidate for enough information to make a well-informed decision.

Never accept an incomplete application from a potential employee. Many applicants prefer to fill out basic information, such as name, phone number, and address and attach a résumé to the application. It is a mistake to accept this incomplete form. The candidate's résumé contains what *he or she wants you* to know; your application asks what *you need* to know. Sound company policy dictates that every applicant fill out the same application from entry level to the top position. Some positions will need supplemental information sheets that address job specific situations.

A well-written application also obtains authorization for checking court records and verifying the applicant's educational history and other credentials. As part of the application process, the applicant should be asked for all appropriate business or professional references and specific written permission to contact them. Full and adequate permission, obtained in advance, reduces the risk of the job seeker accusing a prospective employer of invasion of privacy.

Sources of References

Most candidates can provide several hand-picked references. If you settle for these hand-picked references, such as ministers, prominent community members, government officials, or family friends, you will only get a vague and rose-colored picture of candidate. While these individuals may have a great deal of credibility, they usually do not know the applicant in a work setting and can provide little, if any, real information about job performance. Go beyond hand-picked references to find the real facts about job performance and the behavior that affects it.

These individuals will best know the applicant's real work history.

- Former bosses
- Peers, such as other department heads or team members at each position
- Fellow members of professional associations
- Customers of the company with whom the candidate worked
- Suppliers to the companies for which the candidate worked
- Acquaintances at work
- Former teachers or professors

Supervisors of the candidate, especially during the past five years or at least three positions, are especially important references. For higher level or more critical positions, it is important to delve deeper to understand the applicant's entire work background. Any suspicious information or "red flags" should be investigated, no matter how old they are.

Seek out those who best know the specific duties and responsibilities of the applicant, the actual work conditions under which the job was performed. The purpose of your inquiry is to determine the actual level of performance compared to company standards and others doing the same job.

Number of References

The reason to have an ample number of references is to verify or cross-check facts. For example, if only one or two references are checked, a court could hold that a prospective employer should have known the information from a single reference was false and the employer could be held liable. Checking multiple references is one of the surest ways to avoid charges of negligent hiring. If three references, rather than one, say a former employee was fired for stealing, the prospective employer is on far safer ground denying the applicant employment. By contacting an adequate number of references, you can more accurately judge the reliability of information received and demonstrate that reasonable care was taken in the hiring process.

3 x 3 Rule

To get beyond the hand-picked references and find the truth, you must have multiple sources of information. For years in my workshops, I have recommended using what I call the "3 x 3 Rule." This term refers to obtaining at least three references in each of three key areas:

- Former bosses or supervisors
- Peers at key companies
- Subordinates (if in management) or customers (if in customer contact)

This careful checking will provide a minimum of nine different references that enable you to check beyond the hand-picked three.

One of our clients has taken the 3 x 3 Rule further. Once the applicants have passed the screening interviews and pre-employment checks, at the last in-depth interview they are asked to complete reference worksheets. On these worksheets, the individuals provide detailed information about their last four positions. The requested information includes company names, dates of employment, exact job titles, supervisors' names and titles, supervisors' phone numbers, and how long each individual supervised the candidate. Three supervisors and one other reference for each of the last four companies provide up to sixteen references from which to choose.

After completing the reference worksheets, the applicants sign a statement that the information furnished is accurate, complete, and provided in the pursuit of employment. They acknowledge that misrepresentation or omission in providing information to verify background and employment history is cause for rejection, and, if hired, that misrepresentation or omission discovered later is cause for dismissal from employment. This release also authorizes the investigation of all statements contained in the application and in the worksheet.

Contacting References

All references should be contacted before any job offer is made. In the event that it is impossible to check references at a current employer, an offer can be made contingent on satisfactory completion of reference checks. If sufficient negative information is discovered, the contingent offer can be withdrawn. If the offer is withdrawn, however, the applicant can reasonably infer it was because of something learned during the reference check at the current employer. If possible, avoid this situation, because it can open the door to an allegation of wrongful denial of employment.

Now is the time to verify the information received during the entire employment process and answer the questions, "Can they do the job?" "Do they want to do the job?" and "Will they fit in?" To answer these questions, you need to understand actual job performance.

Not only must you understand the responsibilities, duties, and job performance, you must also understand the conditions under which the individual performed. It is key to know if they took over a position with everything going well and simply continued, or if they took on a difficult or problem situation and improved it dramatically. You're also seeking important information about how they compared to company expectations, and budget, and to others with similar skills and income.

Preparation

Before calling references, it is important to take time to review the candidate's background and what was learned during the interview. Identify any "red flags" or concerns that need to be clarified. Be sure to verify other information. Develop a comfort level that what was provided in the employment process is accurate. Then you can select or create the questions to ask the reference. It's especially helpful to ask the same questions or similar questions of all the references to compare responses. This consistency allows a much more accurate and measured comparison. Typically, some of the questions will be

- How long have you known the candidate?
- What were the specific dates of employment?
- What were *your* position and responsibilities during the candidate's employment?
- What were the candidate's position and responsibilities during employment?
- How would you characterize the candidate's work?
- How did the candidate get along with people? Peers? Upper management? Customers?
- What were the candidate's strengths? Weaknesses?
- What would you suggest the candidate improve to increase chances of success?
- What was the candidate's specific reason for leaving?
- Would you rehire the candidate? Why? Has anyone ever been rehired? Why?

It is important to probe the potential for rehire thoroughly. Some organizations have a no rehire policy, however, many times it is violated for a person with excellent performance. The policy is used to avoid having to go through the employment process and reject an undesirable former employee.

A good way to determine the strictness of the employer's rehire policy is to ask if anyone has ever been rehired. If the answer is yes, then ask under what circumstances the rehire occurred. Asking this question will clarify how the policy is really implemented.

Calling References

When calling references, it is a good idea not call the Personnel or Human Resources Department. They usually know what is in the personnel file, not the real details of the person's performance. In most cases the personnel staff will simply give the equivalent of "name, rank, and serial number." By calling the individual's former supervisor or the owner of the company, you usually get a more candid response. If the employee has been a problem, the supervisor or the owner has a motive to avoid passing on a "bad apple."

It is an excellent idea to avoid using or stressing the word "reference." It is best to say, "John or Mary is in consideration for a position at our organization. He or she suggested I contact you to verify a few facts. May I ask you a few questions?" Using this low-key approach, you have a much greater chance of receiving candid and accurate information.

If the reference resists, you can suggest the importance of being able to verify the information so that the candidate may be considered for the position. If the reference still does not give the information, your only option is to ask the candidate to contact the reference and personally request he or she provide you with the information needed.

While conducting searches as an executive search consultant, I found getting information from references relatively easy. Only one company, a *Fortune* 500 company, refused to give out any information until they received written verification. After receiving a letter verifying my identity and the need for the information, my questions were readily answered.

"Stonewall" References

Once in a while you will encounter a reference attempting to "stonewall" or to not provide any information at all. This lack of response may be due to simply not wanting to provide information or because there may be negative information about the candidate they do not want to share. An absence of accurate performance data, feedback, and detailed and accurate information about personnel actions can also cause a company representative to be resistant to providing a reference. It is essential that information on a candidate's past performance be verified, and it is preferable to get the information from the original source.

If the reference balks at giving information, explain how important the information is: you need it for the candidate to be considered for this position and you would hate for this job opportunity to be missed because the reference information was not complete. Tell the reference that the candidate seems perfect for the position, but in order for him or her to be considered further, additional information is required. Be sure the reference understands everything that is said is confidential and will not be shared with the candidate.

If the individual still will not give out any information, you may suggest that he or she contact the candidate and get the individual's "express" approval. If all else fails, simply call the candidate and ask for additional references, such as those who are no longer with this particular company who can speak freely. If you can't find someone who can verify the individual's job performance in a company, it is a cause for concern. Remember, no available reference from a past employer is a "red flag." When performance is good, a candidate can find someone who will confidentially share information to verify performance; someone you can speak to privately at home; or someone who has already left the company.

Most likely, there are people who have already left the company who know the candidate's performance. Generally, top-performing individuals know who can verify work performance and are willing to assist you in locating them. Many even have written records from their former organization that specify pay, performance, and promotions. Of course, you must also verify that the applicant's reference who left the company actually worked there, too.

Background Checks

By verifying the individual's background and key facts such as driving history and education credentials, you can supplement what you have learned in the reference checks. Checking to uncover felony convictions or indications of other potential problems can help eliminate those who might pose a threat to employees and customers.

Many organizations find it simpler and easier to outsource these checks to companies that specialize in these areas. For a modest investment, credential and criminal records can be verified. Recently, we checked the felon record, employment dates and title, and education of a candidate in a foreign country for less than $150. That investment is a very small sum to pay for a great deal of security.

Evaluating References

It is critical that references be checked with an open mind. Even after a couple of satisfactory references, it is very important to remain impartial. You never know when you will uncover something that is significant.

On a personal note, while at Xerox a number of years ago, I failed to keep an open mind. In reality, I made my decision before completing the reference checks. As a result of this premature conclusion, I overlooked a small bit of information that should have been questioned and pursued. When checking the reference of a new graduate, I talked with her former high school employer who raved about her work performance and background, with one minor exception. He cautiously offered, "She had gotten with the wrong crowd in high school. However, I am sure when she went to college she corrected that." Because I had already made up my mind, I did not pick up this subtle hint and pursue it further. This small hint should have caused me to probe further. Because I did not keep an open mind, evaluate all the information I had heard, and pursue it until satisfied, I made a very painful hiring mistake and learned the hard way.

Even if former employers reveal little about the individual, such as their job title and length of employment, their tone of voice can be significant. If your intuition says there is a problem, be sure to uncover enough information to clarify any issue or concern—before the individual is hired.

After interviews, pre-employment evaluations, background and reference checks, you should ask the key question: Do you want this person working in your organization or driving a vehicle with your employees as passengers? If the answer is no, no matter how desperately you need a person, pass on this candidate.

At Xerox, when I managed a sales team of ten people, my final test was to ask myself if this applicant could and would pay one-tenth of my mortgage payment each month. In reality, since I didn't have direct sales responsibility or a quota, I could only succeed through the efforts of my individual salespeople. They were responsible for my mortgage and ultimately my success.

The goal and reason for reference and background checks is to validate information gained in the hiring process, to assist in hiring the best people possible, and to avoid possible legal entanglements. Nearly everyone has something in his or her background that is not "perfect," but you must determine if it affects the person's capability to perform the job and potential to work with other employees and customers. Accurate, detailed verification of performance is vital to hiring the right employees.

Author
Biographies

Chad Cook, M.B.A. ●
Chad Cook, Chief Executive Officer of Infinite Learning of
Ohio, is a specialist in training and development.

Chad focuses on organizational design and development
strategies for workforce stability. His extensive experience in
the realm of human resource and organizational development
has produced significant productivity and performance returns for organizations. As the Corporate Director for Human
Resource Development for Rubbermaid Incorporated, Chad
was involved with organizational restructuring, strategic plan
deployment, organizational change management, performance system design, intranet design, and management. For
11 years, Chad worked with Rubbermaid to implement development and performance support programs enabling the
achievement of organizational goals.

More recently, he has worked with companies to introduce
career systems for managers and employees, full-service as-
sessment/planning and deployment programs, key talent retention systems, executive leader development, team design
and skills training, sales training, human resource strate-
gies/skills, and many other systems or programs supporting
workforce stability.

Chad earned a Master of Business Administration in Management Systems from Baldwin-Wallace College in 1985.
His Bachelor of Arts degree was granted in the field of Psychology by Thiel College in 1971.

Chad is a member of the American Society for Training and Development and the Institute of Management Consultants.

Carol D'Amico, Ph.D. •
Dr. Carol D'Amico's specialties include workforce trends, education reform, education policy and analysis, program development and evaluation, and workforce development. She currently serves as Executive Director for Workforce Development at Ivy Tech State College.

Prior to her current position, Carol was a Senior Researcher with the Hudson Institute in Indianapolis. She is co-author of *Workforce 2020*, a book describing the challenges and opportunities for American corporations and workers in the early twenty-first century. In her work with Hudson from 1990 to 1999, she assisted business and government leaders in developing effective ways to improve public education. Carol currently conducts research and advises businesses and communities on strategies to deal with economic and workforce trends.

Before joining Hudson, Carol was a Policy Advisor for the Indiana Superintendent of Public Instruction, focusing on strategies to improve public education. Carol also served as a Senior Program Analyst for the Indiana General Assembly, where she conducted research on state government issues.

Carol was granted her Ph.D. in Leadership and Policy by Indiana University. Her Master of Arts in Adult Education and Organizational Development was earned at Indiana University.

Carol has been cited in numerous publications including *The Wall Street Journal, Business Week, USA Today, Indianapolis Star, Indianapolis Business Journal,* and *Education Week,* and comments frequently on education and workforce issues for local and national television and radio programs. She has also testified before the U.S. Congress and several state legislatures on job training and education issues.

Catherine D. Fyock, CSP, SPHR • • • • • • • • • • • • • • • •
Catherine D. Fyock, CSP, SPHR, is President of Innovative
Management Concepts, a management consulting firm specializing in solutions for recruiting and retaining employees
in an aging and changing workforce. Based in Crestwood,
Kentucky, some of her clients include AT&T, Federal Express, BellSouth, and KFC Corp., as well as numerous local,
state, and national agencies on aging.

Before starting her consulting business, Cathy was Director of Field Human Resources for the Kentucky Fried
Chicken Corporation. She was instrumental in the development of many key programs for recruiting and retaining employees, including *The Colonel's Tradition*—KFC's national
initiative for employing older workers.

A noted lecturer and seminar leader, Cathy is an active
member of the Society for Human Resource Management,
having served as Chair of the National Committee for Training and Development. She has also been President of the
Board of Directors for the Human Resource Certification Institute and is the Immediate Past President of the Consultant's
Forum Board of Directors. She was a member of the Certified
Speaking Professional (CSP) Council for the National Speakers Association and is a past president of her chapter.

Cathy has a Bachelor of Arts degree from Western Ken-
tucky University, and a Master of Arts degree in Personnel
Management from the University of Louisville, where she
taught personnel management. She earned her Certified
Speaking Professional designation in 1993 and is certified as
a Senior Professional in Human Resources (SPHR). The
Louisville SHRM chapter honored her with their first ever
Award for Professional Excellence.

Cathy has authored numerous articles and is a featured
columnist for trade publications. She is the author of *America's Work Force is Coming of Age: What Every Business
Needs to Know to Recruit, Train, Manage, and Retain an*

Aging Work Force; *Get The Best: How to Recruit the People You Want;* and *The Managing Diversity Series* modular training programs. Her newest book, *UnRetirement: A Career Guide for the Retired . . . the Soon-to-Be-Retired . . . the Never-Want-to-Be-Retired*, has been selected as a Fortune Book Club Alternate Selection, is a winner of the Mature Media National Awards, and has been featured in *Business Week* and *WORTH* magazines.

Sylvia K. Gaffney, M.S.O.D. • • • • • • • • • • • • • • • • • •
Sylvia K. Gaffney is President of Gaffney Corporate Strategies and Career Systems, Inc., Rockford, Illinois. Sylvia has 15 years' experience in the staffing and outplacement industries with special expertise as an organization development consultant. Her areas of specialty include custom-designed organizational effectiveness and change management programs. Her firm assists executive leadership, management teams, and human resource departments on a national and international basis in addressing the needs of an organization's current personnel, potential employees, and those individuals whose employment is terminated. In this role, Sylvia facilitates strategic planning sessions, team building initiatives, internal career development programs, retention and succession planning, coaching and mentoring programs, training, testing, third-party exit interviews, orientation programs, and career transition assistance.

Sylvia serves as a member of the Workforce Investment Board and has been very active on an advisory council for the Illinois State Board of Education for Business–Education Partnerships. She currently sits on a regional bank board and served two years as Chairman of the Board of a northern Illinois chamber of commerce. She is a Fellow and Charter Member of the International Association of Career Management Professionals and serves as an adjunct faculty member at the Baxter Institute and for the Society for Human Resource Management.

Sylvia holds three master's degrees. Her most recent is her Master of Science degree in Organizational Development granted by Pepperdine University. Her other graduate degrees are in Curriculum Design and Educational Administration. Sylvia's Bachelor of Science degree was granted by Rockford College.

Sylvia brings a unique perspective to retention work. During the past 15 years, she has been involved in three separate industries, in addition to owning and operating a successful staffing company and an outplacement and organizational development consulting firm

Sylvia has authored a career development book that will be released in Spring 2000.

Joyce L. Gioia, M.B.A., CMC • • • • • • • • • • • • • • • • • • •

Joyce L. Gioia is President of The Herman Group, a firm of Certified Management Consultants based in Greensboro, North Carolina. Her areas of specialty include internal and external marketing, workforce and workplace trends, and performance-directed inspiration.

Joyce's background includes experience in sales and management in several industries, including personnel staffing. At 28, she was named publisher of a national consumer magazine. Later, as a nationally recognized marketing consultant, Joyce achieved significant success in direct marketing, new product launches, and arranging strategic alliances. As a marketing consultant, her clients included AT&T, ABC, and Bloomingdales. For years she served as one of the judges for the prestigious Echo Awards in the direct marketing industry.

Joyce is frequently quoted in both print and broadcast media as a recognized specialist on relationships in the world of business. She was featured on the Lifetime Cable Network television program, *New Attitudes,* and has been quoted in numerous periodicals including *Business Week, Entrepreneur, Fast Company, USA TODAY,* and the *Christian Science Monitor.* She is also a frequent speaker at association and corporate conventions throughout the United States and has spoken in several other countries as well. More than 10,000 subscribers in three dozen countries read the e-mailed weekly advisory on trends, *Trend Alert*, written by Joyce and her partner, Roger Herman.

Fordham University awarded Joyce a Master of Business Administration degree in 1976. Her Bachelor of Arts degree was granted, with a major in languages, by the University of Denver. She also holds a master's degree in Theology and a master's degree in Spiritual Counseling from The New Seminary in New York City.

The Institute of Management Consultants granted Joyce the designation of Certified Management Consultant (CMC), the highest accreditation awarded in the management consulting profession. She is an active member of the Institute and a professional member of both the National Speakers Association and The World Future Society. Joyce is also a member of the American Society for Training and Development.

Joyce is a co-author of *Lean & Meaningful: A New Culture for Corporate America* (1998) and *How to Become an Employer of Choice* (2000). She is also the author of *Add Value & Thrive: Survival Tactics for the New Millennium* (2000).

Brian W. Grossman, Ph.D. ●
Brian W. Grossman is a clinician and trainer specializing in organizational development. His specific focus is working with employers—particularly managers and supervisors—to support them in facilitating stronger performance from underachievers. Brian is based in Miami Beach, Florida.

In his career, Brian has worked with employees, children, adolescents, and adults to enhance the performance of underachievers. He is known for his expertise in assessment and consultative training to achieve change. As Senior Psychologist coordinating outpatient mental health at a maximum-security prison (supervising seven master's-level therapists), Brian gained considerable experience and insight into how people outside society's mainstream can be supported to become productive members of their community. Over the years, he has also gained significant experience in therapy, counseling, and change management for individuals, groups, and organizations.

Brian earned his Bachelor of Arts degree in Psychology from California State University at Northridge in 1984, then continued his education at the California School of Professional Psychology in Los Angeles. That institution granted him a Master of Arts degree in Clinical Psychology in 1986 and a Doctor of Philosophy degree in the field in 1989.

Brian is a member of the National Speakers Association, the American Psychological Association, and the American Society for Training and Development.

Roger E. Herman, CSP, CMC ••••••••••••••••••••

Roger Herman is Chief Executive Officer of The Herman Group, a firm of Certified Management Consultants based in Greensboro, North Carolina. His areas of specialty include organizational development, corporate culture change, workforce and workplace trends, employee retention, and emerging leadership styles.

Prior to founding his consulting firm in 1980, Roger gained more than 18 years of experience in sales and management in manufacturing, distribution, retail, and professional service organizations. His public sector experience includes service as a City Manager and a municipal Director of Public Works. During the Viet Nam era, he served as a Counterintelligence Special Agent for the U.S. Army.

Roger earned a Bachelor of Arts in Sociology from Hiram College (1965) and a Master of Arts in Public Administration from The Ohio State University (1977). The National Speakers Association awarded him the designation of Certified Speaking Professional (CSP); he is also recognized as a Certified Management Consultant (CMC) by the Institute of Management Consultants, the highest accreditation awarded in the management consulting profession. Roger is one of only 15 people in the world to hold both designations.

Active in the Institute of Management Consultants, Roger is a member of the Board of Directors and serves as Vice Chair of the professional organization. He is also active in the National Speakers Association, the Society for Human Resource Management, and the World Future Society. He serves as Contributing Editor for Workforce and Workplace Trends for *The Futurist* magazine and as a subject matter expert on workforce issues for Aftermarketnews.com. He is Senior Fellow of the Workforce Stability Institute.

Roger's articles are frequently published in trade magazines and professional journals. He is frequently cited by journalists in such publications as *The Wall Street Journal*, *Fast Company*, *Entrepreneur*, *Human Resource Executive*, and *Workforce*. His syndicated column, "Future@Work," is carried by a number of trade publications. More than 10,000 subscribers in three dozen countries read his e-mailed weekly advisory on trends, *Trend Alert*.

Roger's books include *How to Become an Employer of Choice*; *How to Choose Your Next Employer*; *Signs of the Times*; *Keeping Good People*; *Lean & Meaningful: A New Culture for Corporate America*; *The Process of Excelling*; *Turbulence!*; *Emergency Operations Plan;* and *Disaster Planning for Local Government*. A new book, *Micro to Maestro*, is scheduled for publication in the Fall of 2000. He also produced a six-tape audio album titled *Keeping Good People*, a number of single cassette audiotapes, an educational package entitled "Keeping Winners," and a management training program on employee retention.

Julie A. Moreland, CMC •
Julie A. Moreland is President of Jobfun.com, an Atlanta, Georgia, consulting firm providing advice, products, and support services in the field of job fit competency measurement and performance management. Her fields of specialty are as-

sessment technologies, intellectual capital diagnostics, team engineering, and pre-employment systems design. Most recently, Julie assisted in the development of new Assessment Technologies specifically designed for the Internet.

Julie is a nationally respected authority on practical business applications of assessment technologies. She also developed considerable financial and management expertise during the past 15 years in diverse business situations. As a high level manager in a $5 billion, 160-branch division of a Fortune 100 company, Julie gained a perspective on the complex workings of a major corporation. She then ventured into the challenging world of high tech entrepreneurship as the vice president of a $4 million start-up computer solutions company.

As an individual entrepreneur, Julie successfully started and grew her own business. In 1992, she merged her firm with The Russell Group and became the president. That firm was developed and sold. She then formed a company, Moreland Russell, Inc., with her partner Chuck Russell. Most recently, they formed Jobfun.com, positioned to develop and deliver assessment technology to the Internet.

Julie holds a Bachelor of Arts degree in Business Administration/Computer Information Systems from the University of West Georgia. The Institute of Management Consultants recognizes her as a Certified Management Consultant (CMC), the highest accreditation awarded in the management consulting profession. She serves as the president of the Board of Visitors for the University of West Georgia School of Business.

Julie is the co-developer of several assessment products including CheckStart™, a pre-employment system; teentrack™, a career tool for young adults; and CareerMinder™, a career tool for adults.

Billy C. Mullins II, M.S. •••••••••••••••••••••••
Billy C. Mullins II, is President and Chief Executive Officer of the Vikus Corporation, based in Chattanooga, Tennessee.

His areas of specialty include job/duty analysis, employee selection systems, performance appraisal systems, and human resource measurements.

Billy uses human resource measurement systems to improve employee performance and workforce stability. He believes that the foundation of human resource management is job analysis. Billy has developed a unique and effective job analysis process using structured interviews, observation, and proprietary software. This process can be used to gather and organize job data to support eight different human resource (HR) functions.

In the selection arena, Billy developed Vikus's Computer-Aided Interview, which has enabled some companies to reduce their new hire turnover by more than 50 percent. Believing that "what gets measured, gets done," Billy's company provides systems to measure both human resource management functions and employee performance.

Billy's senior management experience (for one of the nation's largest snack food manufacturers) in both operations and human resources, has given him unique and very practical insights that can help HR departments play a major role in helping organizations achieve their strategic objectives.

Billy holds a Bachelor of Arts degree in Theology from Southern Adventist University (1986) and a Master of Science degree in Industrial/Organizational Psychology from the University of Tennessee at Chattanooga (1994).

Bob Nelson, M.B.A. •
Bob Nelson is Founder and President of Nelson Motivation, Inc. in San Diego, California. His specialty is employee recognition and motivation that leads to higher productivity, inspired leadership, and more effective management.

Bob is a best-selling business author. His books, *1001 Ways to Reward Employees* and *1001 Ways to Energize Employees*, have been on the *Business Week* best-seller list for more than four years. *1001 Ways to Reward Employees* has sold more than one million copies. Bob's newest book is *1001 Ways to Take Initiative at Work*. Bob was selected by *Time* magazine to be its "staff management expert" for the new TIME Vista Boardroom, an interactive business web site.

As a speaker, Bob provides a unique blend of insight, application, and inspiration that motivates listeners to want to take positive action. Both thoughtful and thought-provoking, he challenges listeners to examine their beliefs and practices in order to improve.

Bob Nelson is a former vice president at Blanchard Training & Development and has worked as a management trainer for Norwest Bank and Control Data Corporation. He holds an M.B.A. from the University of California, Berkeley, and is a doctoral candidate in the Executive Management Program of the Peter F. Drucker Graduate Management Center at The Claremont Graduate University in suburban Los Angeles, California.

Bob is a member of the National Speakers Association and the founder of the National Association for Employee Recognition. He has written two other books, *Managing For Dummies* and *Consulting For Dummies*.

Wayne Outlaw, CSP, CMC •••••••••••••••••••••

Wayne Outlaw is President of OUTLAW GROUP, Inc. of Mt. Pleasant, South Carolina. His area of specialty is strategic staffing systems that ensure companies have adequate human capital to acquire, serve, and keep customers. These customized systems define job requirements; identify attributes of high performers; establish candidate benchmarks; develop corporate-wide recruiting systems; define the staffing process; integrate pre-employment selection tools; and develop the interviewing and reference checking skills necessary to manage the staffing process just as other key strategic objectives are managed.

Wayne is author of the critically acclaimed *Smart Staffing: How to Hire, Reward, and Keep Top Employees for Your*

Growing Company (Upstart Publishing Company, 1998). *Smart Staffing* is an extremely versatile book with uses ranging from a human resource desk reference for small businesses, to a textbook for human resource courses at colleges such as UCLA. It is being translated and will be published shortly in the People's Republic of China.

Wayne is one of less than 15 individuals to have ever been certified both as a Certified Speaking Professional (CSP) by the National Speakers Association and a Certified Management Consultant (CMC) by the Institute of Management Consultants. He has been acknowledged by *The Wall Street Journal* as a "staffing expert" and is quoted in publications such as *Fast Company, Nation's Business, Investors Business Daily*, and *Entrepreneur Magazine*. His clients range from small entrepreneurial, high-growth companies to *Fortune* 500 organizations such as American Express, Procter & Gamble, and Morgan Stanley Dean Witter.

Wayne developed the benchmark sales strategy used worldwide by Xerox to beat lower-priced competition. He is a 1967 graduate of The Citadel. He is an active member of the Institute of Management Consultants and the National Speakers Association.

In addition to the book *Smart Staffing*, Wayne has developed Web courses: "Smart Staffing," "Recruiting in a Tight Labor Market," and "Performance-Based Selection," as well as audio learning systems: *Total Customer Service*; *Management: Solving the People Puzzle*; *Total Time Management*; and *Hire the Winners*.

Chuck Russell •
Chuck Russell is the Senior Partner of Jobfun.com, an Atlanta, Georgia, consulting firm. He is the leading authority on the application of new assessment technologies to business practices such as performance management, recruiting programs, selection systems, work group analysis, team en-

gineering, and process design. With a library of hundreds of assessment products and experience with hundreds more, he provides comparative analyses on such products for businesses, law firms, and consultants alike.

Chuck is the author of *Right Person—Right Job, Guess or Know*. In 1996, this ground-breaking book shattered the existing paradigms of hiring, training, and people management by showing how research with new assessment technology could analyze and often predict job performance. It remains the primer for using assessment instruments in business practices.

Chuck has continued to pioneer much of the thought leadership in the area of differentiating between the elastic and non-elastic competencies that determine performance within work groups. This knowledge is critical to managing workforce stability and to optimizing any group's performance. Chuck's approach is practical, pragmatic, and passionate about the potential of people. His speaking style has been described as part humorist and part Southern evangelist.

Chuck holds a Bachelor of Arts degree in Economics from Spring Hill College. He is a member of the Institute of Management Consultants. Chuck is also the Small Business Expert on people issues for www.smartonline.com, the leading Web site for small business owners and managers.

His next book, *Managing with the Lights On*, is scheduled for publication in the Spring of 2000.

Marion Smalle, Ph.D., LL.B. • • • • • • • • • • • • • • • • • •
Marion Smalle is a management consultant based in Greensboro, North Carolina. Her specialty is building commitment and dedication among front-line employees to generate greater productivity and longevity.

Born and raised in South Africa, Marion earned a degree in teaching from Rand Afrikaans University in Johannesburg, South Africa. She then attended the University of the Witwatersrand in Johannesburg where she obtained an

Honor's degree, a Master's degree, and a Ph.D. in Education. She continued her studies at the same university and completed her law degree (LL.B.) in 1986.

During her years as a part time student after obtaining her teaching degree, she worked in the training and development field in South African organizations, one of which had 26,000 employees. It was during this time that she developed a front-line training program that proved to be a great success. In 1980, she started her own training company called Training for Africa, and through the success of this company, engaged in training and development work in 16 countries. Today she consults and provides training for American employers interested in building more cohesive, enlightened, and stable workforces.

Marion is a member of the Institute of Management Consultants, the Society for Human Resource Management, and the American Society for Training and Development.

Recommended Reading

These books can be ordered conveniently at the website of The Workforce Stability Institute. Simply go to www.employee.org and click on Recommended Reading.

Adler, Lou. *Hire with Your Head.*

Blohowiak, Don. *Your People are Your Product.*

Catlette, Bill, and Richard Hadden. *Contented Cows Give Better Milk.*

Dauten, Dale A. *The Gifted Boss: How to Find, Create and Keep Great Employees.*

Fyock, Catherine D. *America's Work Force is Coming of Age: What Every Business Needs to Know to Recruit, Train, Manage, and Retain an Aging Work Force.*

Fyock, Catherine D. *Get the Best: How to Recruit the People You Want.*

Fyock, Catherine D. *UnRetirement: A Career Guide for the Retired . . . the Soon-to-Be-Retired . . . the Never-Want-to-Be-Retired.*

Harris, Jim. *Getting Employees to Fall in Love with Your Company.*

Harris, Jim, and Joan Brannick. *Finding and Keeping Great People.*

Herman, Roger E. *Keeping Good People*.

Herman, Roger E. *The Process of Excelling*.

Herman, Roger E. *Signs of the Times*.

Herman, Roger E., and Joyce L. Gioia. *Lean & Meaningful*.

Judy, Richard W., and Carol D'Amico. *Workforce 2020*.

Kaye, Beverly, and Sharon Jordan-Evans. *Love 'Em or Lose 'Em: Getting Good People to Stay*.

Massmer, Max. *The Fast Forward MBA in Hiring: Finding and Keeping the Best People*.

Mornell, Pierre. *45 Effective Ways for Hiring Smart*.

Nelson, Bob. *1001 Ways to Energize Employees*.

Nelson, Bob. *1001 Ways to Reward Employees*.

Nelson, Bob. *1001 Ways to Take Initiative at Work*.

Outlaw, Wayne. *Smart Staffing*.

Pinsker, Richard. *Hiring Winners*.

Russell, Chuck. *Right Person-Right Job, Guess or Know*.

Schaffer, William A. *High-Tech Careers for Low-Tech People*.

Swan, William S. *How to Pick the Right People*.

Winninger, Tom. *Hiring Smart*.

Yate, Martin. *Keeping the Best*.

The Workforce Stability Institute

The Workforce Stability Institute is a not-for-profit organization dedicated to research and education in the recruiting, optimizing, and retaining of employees in corporations, not-for-profit organizations, and government entities.

The Institute was founded by consultants who specialize in various aspects of finding and keeping qualified workers. Watching the trends, they became highly sensitive to the fact that these vital tasks were becoming increasingly difficult.

Clients and consultants had some of the solutions to the problem, but no one had all the answers. With the intensifying labor shortage, these clients and consultants saw a need to bring together as much information as possible—in a way that as many people as possible could benefit from what everyone else was doing. The need was clear: research, sharing, and education were essential for continued economic health.

The director and staff are responsible for coordinating the day-to-day business of the Institute. Professional members of the organization are known as Fellows of the Institute. These specialists are responsible for leading the research, monitoring the field, and providing educational and informational services to the Institute's clients and the world at-large. Each Fellow has particular expertise in one or more areas relating to the work of the Institute.

The Workforce Stability Institute publishes a monthly newsletter, *Workforce Stability Alert*. In addition, an "open forum" on the Internet is offered as a public service. Interested participants may register through the Institute's web site at www.employee.org.

The Workforce Stability Institute also produces an 8-page monthly newsletter to help human resource professionals and business executives attract, optimize, and hold onto their good people. This newsletter is called the *The Workforce Stability Alert* and it is published by M. Lee Smith Publishers in Nashville, Tennessee. To receive a FREE copy, call 800-274-5094 and mention that you saw the offer in the book.

> The Workforce Stability Institute
> 3400 Willow Grove Court
> Greensboro, NC 27410-8600
> Voice   (336) 282-1480
> Fax   (336) 282-2003
> admin@employee.org

Index

J

L

M

N

O

P

R

Herman, Roger E.   HF5549.5
Workforce stability: your   H551w
competitive edge

DEMCO